TO: J &
Chris

MW01075195

BEST-KEPT
BOY
IN THE WORLD
BY ARTHUR VANDERBILT

MAGNUS BOOKS

Copyright © 2014 by Arthur Vanderbilt

Magnus Books
An Imprint of Riverdale Avenue Books
5676 Riverdale Ave., Suite 101
Bronx, NY 10471

All rights reserved. No part of this book may be reproduced or transmitted in any form or by any means, electronic or mechanical, including photocopying, without permission in writing from the publisher.

Printed in the United States of America

First Edition

Layout by www.formatting4U.com
Cover by: Nick Vogelson, Townhouse Creative

Print ISBN: 978-1936833-41-2
Digital ISBN: 978-1-62601-125-0

www.magnusbooks.com
www.RiverdaleAvenueBooks.com

CONTENTS

FOREWORD

It was a pity, Gore Vidal once remarked, that Denham Fouts never wrote a memoir. For Vidal, Denny was *"un homme fatal."*[1]

Truman Capote found that "to watch him walk into a room was an experience. He was beyond being good-looking; he was the single most charming-looking person I've ever seen."[2] Capote loved to conjecture that "had Denham Fouts yielded to Hitler's advances there would have been no World War Two."[3]

Jimmie Daniels, the nightclub singer who performed at his own Harlem club that bore his name, thought Denny "was about the most beautiful boy anybody had ever seen. His skin always looked as if it had just been scrubbed; it seemed to have no pores at all, it was so smooth."[4]

To King Paul of Greece he was "my dear Denham" or "Darling Denham," and the King's telegrams to Denny from the Royal Palace always were signed "love, Paul."[5]

Peter Watson, the wealthy financial backer of the popular British literary magazine *Horizon*, had an erection whenever he was in the same room with Denny.[6]

The artist Michael Wishart met Denny for the first time at a party in Paris and realized instantly he was in love and that "the only place in the world I wanted to be was in Denham's bedroom."[7]

FOREWORD

Best-selling author Glenway Wescott thought Denny "absolutely enchanting and ridiculously good-looking ... He had the most delicious body odor; I once swiped one of his handkerchiefs."[8]

Lord Tredegar, one of the largest landowners in Great Britain, saw Denny being led by the police through the lobby of an expensive hotel on Capri, convinced the police to let him pay the bills Denny owed, and then took Denny to accompany him and his wife as they continued on their tour of the world.

Novelist Christopher Isherwood, who Denny considered his best friend, called him "the most expensive male prostitute in the world."

Today, someone who projects such an instant and potent power of attraction could forge a successful career, perhaps as a male model, as a character in a daytime soap opera, as a tabloid celebrity, as a television or movie star, maybe even as an acclaimed actor. But Denny was born in 1914 in Jacksonville, Florida, when such options were not yet available to those rare individuals endowed with this sort of sexual magnetism. He never did write a memoir that would have told his strange story, that may have explained how it felt to possess those magical powers, to occupy the thoughts of another, to become the obsession of their lives, to live well off of their wealth and infatuation. How would it feel to be Aschenbach's Tadzio in Thomas Mann's *Death in Venice*? To be Humbert's Lolita in Nabokov's masterpiece? Jay Gatsby's Daisy in *The Great Gatsby*?

"The mass of men," Thoreau was brave enough and honest enough to write in *Walden*, "lead lives of quiet desperation." Most of us come, go, and are gone, our lives lived in shades of gray no more distinguishable, no more memorable, than the squirrels in a park on a coming of winter morning. Denny was one of those rare individuals who, whatever his faults, brought color into the black and white etchings of everyday life.

FOREWORD

Denny never did write his own story, but he does move through many memoirs of the times. And for some of the most renowned authors of those times, he was a muse, and that color he brought into a squirrel-gray world inspired them to capture him in their prose. Denny is "Paul" in Christopher Isherwood's *Down There on a Visit*. He is a character in Gore Vidal's novel *The Judgment of Paris*, and in his short story "Pages from an Abandoned Journal." He appears in Truman Capote's infamous *Answered Prayers* on which the author was working, or not working, when he died. Denny was proud to find himself a character in Somerset Maugham's *The Razor's Edge*.

To be immortalized in a story by a famed author would be enough to earn a footnote in literary history. To have inspired the body of work Denham Fouts did is to become a legend. Who was this man, this enigma, who died at thirty-four, whose looks and personality so charmed and intrigued some of the wealthiest men and some of the most celebrated authors of the twentieth century? This is his story.

CHAPTER ONE

"UN HOMME FATAL"

It had been a long six years since Peter Watson sent Denny to the United States as the Nazis marched toward Paris. Denny had made his way to California, lived in Santa Monica with Christopher Isherwood with whom he practiced Eastern mysticism, became a conscientious objector and served in a forestry camp, and was studying to become a psychiatrist. Now, at last, in the spring of 1946, as weary and war-wounded Europe was beginning to recover, Denny returned to Paris, heading straight to Peter Watson's apartment at 44 Rue du Bac.

It was a "sombre faubourg apartment with the eighteenth century windows," as one friend described it,[1] where, in paneled rooms that before the War had been filled with sculptures and antiques, Watson had hung the modern masterworks he had been acquiring, a collection of what he felt were the most significant paintings of each of the artists he was collecting, the best of de Chirico, Gris, Klee, Miro, and Picasso. Six servants had managed the enormous apartment which was in an elegant eighteenth century townhouse right off the Boulevard Saint Germain, close to the Seine. It was set back from the street with a private garden behind it, and through the large windows and French doors leading out to a terrace was—Paris: the Eiffel Tower, the Grand Palais, the roof of the Louvre, the Sacre Coeur, and not far away, Notre Dame and the Jardin du Luxemburg.

Peter had not been prepared for what he found when, after the War, he and his friend, the famed literary critic and essayist Cyril Connolly, returned to Paris in July 1945. When they unlocked and opened the door, they were shocked. "My flat's a shambles", Peter wrote to a friend "—really heartbreaking and so filthy."[2] His extraordinary art collection (which today would have been valued at hundreds of millions of dollars) had disappeared. What furniture remained was broken, dirty draperies hung in shreds, everything of value was missing, including what little he had hidden before evacuating as the Nazi tanks approached the city. Connolly found the once grand quarters "very dilapidated and buggery"[3] and "terribly depressing, empty of everything, no hot water, no clean sheets ...My bed is a sofa in the dining room— nowhere to unpack anything, and I have to go through Peter's room whenever I want to go to the bathroom. It is so strange that Peter, who once had a genius for gracious living, now comes to symbolize morbid discomfort to me."[4] For Connolly the flat was "heavily mined" with reminders of his ex-wife Jean; there, still hanging where Jean and Denny had nailed it for Christmas in 1938, was a scraggly piece of dried out mistletoe.[5]

Discouraged, depressed by what he found and did not find, Peter nevertheless had worked to prepare the apartment for a party, a special party to celebrate the return to Paris, to him, after six years of separation, the love of his life, his obsession: Denham Fouts.

One of the guests at Peter's party that evening was Michael Wishart, the seventeen-year-old grandson of Colonel Sidney Wishart, who had been the Sheriff of London, the son of Ernest Wishart, who owned an estate in Sussex near the sea, and of the sophisticated, glamorous, free-spirited Lorna, who gave birth to Michael when she was seventeen, and who, whenever possible, sped away from her husband's estate in her chocolate brown Bentley, racing straight for London's nightclubs and a series of lovers.

Michael Wishart would become an artist, a painter of some renown, a precocious talent who was selling his paintings when he was fourteen and had his first exhibition in London, and a well received exhibition at that, at the Archer Gallery at the age of sixteen. He was, in fact, precocious in many respects. Michael was twelve when Great Britain declared war on Germany and Messerschmitts began flying over the English Channel. Those occasional German aviators who managed to parachute from their stricken fighters were captured and put to work by the English. One, not much older than Michael, "blonde and arrogant, the incarnation of a Hitler Youth poster,"[6] was brought to work on Michael's family's estate. Michael found intriguingly irresistible this sullen POW named Harm, and when no one was watching, began bringing him small gifts—cigarettes, chocolates, beer. At that age, Michael already was quite handsome with his thick dark hair and eyebrows, seductive eyes and mouth, cleft chin, baritone voice. He and the foreign laborer could communicate only by glances, but those glances soon became more meaningful and Michael thought he could read in them that "he would follow wherever I led."[7] Michael was correct. One day, as Michael was seated by a stone wall sketching a landscape, the German youth came and sat down next to him. Michael walked with him through the orchards, past classical statuary, through gates in walls and hedges, across fields to an abandoned shed, and there "we made a private truce without waiting for the general armistice to be declared, for which I feel toward him nothing but gratitude."[8] It must have been quite a private armistice with Harm. Forty years later, and an extremely sexually active four decades they were, Michael would write that "I have never since experienced physical desire comparable to that which I felt for the German POW."[9] He added that "thanks to him, and his silk parachute, I can say that homosexuality came to me, quite literally, 'out of the blue.'"[10] At the time, though, Michael was alarmed about what he had done and about what he was feeling, and wasted no time seeking a psychiatrist to determine what was wrong with him and to cure him. After a number of unsatisfying sessions, the psychiatrist left him with these words: "Well, old fellow, remember that variety is the spice of life."[11]

Truly words to live by. And live by them Michael did. Throughout his life, his affairs with women were as passionate as those with men, and he moved back and forth between the sexes and between partners with abandon.

The onset of the War created for Michael something of a holiday atmosphere, a time, like summer vacation, when society's rules seemed to go by the wayside. Whenever school was out, he traveled to London. By day, he pursued his art and met other artists. By night, the streets of London were black, an inky darkness shattered by the wail of air raid sirens, by bursts of batteries of anti-aircraft artillery, by the fearsome drone of the doodle bugs, the whine and thud of bombs, ambulance sirens, fire engines racing to conflagrations. Stephen Spender remembered "streets full of glass like heaped-up ice, the fires making a great sunset beyond the silhouette of Saint Paul's, the East End houses collapsed like playing cards."[12] The basement clubs and pubs—the Sunset, the Moon Glow, the Caribbean—served as shelters for Londoners, and a youth of Michael's age was as welcome as anyone, was served liquor like anyone, could buy marijuana like anyone. Everyone knew that the next bomb could be a direct hit, and Michael found that as a result "everyone dropped his inhibitions and prejudices in the gutter, where they belong, and indulged in a non-stop *danse macabre.*"[13]

Michael was in his element. In the clubs he met pimps and prostitutes, phony "counts" who claimed they were kings, Dylan Thomas measuring his penis with a ruler to an admiring audience of ladies interested in poetry. "Tin hats and gas masks were worn, which resembled those beauty products to be found in the sex shops of Amsterdam."[14] Michael became something of a favorite of the clubs' habitués. Whenever he came down the grand staircase of the Gargoyle Club at 69 Dean Street in Soho, the band leader would strike up his favorite song, "Stay as Sweet as You Are," and Michael would dance with Pauline, the daughter of the Club's owner:

"Stay as sweet as you are,
Don't let a thing ever change you.
Stay as sweet as you are.
Don't let a soul rearrange you."

Through his artist friends, Michael had met Peter Watson who soon became his first patron. When seventeen-year-old Michael found himself in Paris in July of 1946, Peter invited him to his party for Denny.

Michael arrived at 44 Rue du Bac as the grand salon was filling with men "and their expensive-looking toy-friends" and "champagne bottles were exploding, punctuating the familiar shrill chatter of the parrot house."[15] All that was missing was the guest of honor, that legend from the pre-war party scene in Europe. The usually unflappable Peter seemed concerned, then annoyed, then agitated, shouting at Denny who had locked himself in the bedroom. The evening wore on. "Some unsteady American boys whom I had no wish to know better were drenching one another with soda siphons, laughing inanely."[16] Guests started drifting away, and finally, disgusted, Peter stalked out. Michael alone stayed, perhaps hoping finally to meet the infamous Mr. Fouts, perhaps because, young and alone in the city, he had nowhere else to go.

He began admiring the salon, running his hands over the paneling, looking out the tall windows at the city of Paris.

While lost in thought, the bedroom door swung open. There stood Denham Fouts.

To Michael, he appeared to be about twenty-one. "In other circumstances one would have imagined him to be the best-looking boy at a West Coast college. He wore nothing but cream-coloured flannel trousers and had the torso of an athlete. Along his beautiful shoulders and golden forearms ran snow-white mice with startled pink eyes, which he stroked with the backs of his hands."[17] It was vintage Denny.

"Trotsky," Denny called, and an enormous black dog gamboled in and "rubbed a dark head against Denham's pale, flannel thighs,"[18] the dog Denny had adopted while doing service as a conscientious objector at a forestry camp outside Los Angeles. Side by side, Denny and Trotsky walked back into the paneled bedroom, illuminated only by a small, orange-shaded oil lamp set in the center of a large bed. Mesmerized, Michael followed. Over the bed hung a painting, an oil by Pavel Tchelitchev, the Russian émigré artist who at the time was collected as avidly as Picasso, Matisse, Léger, Dali, and Rouault. It was a life-size canvas of a naked Adonis, painted from the perspective of between his splayed legs with the focus on the crotch. Sometimes Denny hung this on the ceiling over his bed, sometimes he hung it upside down.

Denny stretched luxuriously across the bed, and, as Michael watched, picked up an opium pipe, impaled an opium pill with a gold needle, and mashed it around the base of the pipe's bowl, then heated the pipe over the oil lamp on the bed, inhaled the smoke deeply and held his inhalation as long as he could. He tapped the pipe into a dish on the floor next to the bed to satisfy Trotsky's addiction. It must have been quite a scene for a young artist's eyes: "Lit from beneath, his handsome Pacific face assumed the air of a Mandarin prince."[19]

In his memoirs, Michael noted that he had been in love three times in his life and that on average it took him about forty-five minutes to realize it. That night, he beat the averages.

"Don't go. I don't want to be alone tonight," were the

first words Denny spoke in his magnetic voice of midnight, Denny's first acknowledgement that someone else was there.

Michael sat down on the bed beside him, and, noticing how beautiful his bare feet were, held his ankle. Denny heated another opium pill in his pipe and handed the jade mouthpiece of the pipe to Michael.

"Now inhale hard," he instructed.

The teenager did exactly as told and rushed to the bathroom to vomit into the mauve marble sink with its gold swan-head faucets.

But Michael came back to the bed, and tried again. The next time was better. Much better.

Denny put some long playing records on a turntable. He drank half a bottle of whiskey. He paged through the *Herald Tribune* to check the financial markets. He showed Michael a telegram he had received that read: "HAPPY BIRTHDAY LOVE PAUL."

"Know who that's from?" Denny asked Michael. "The King of Greece. He never forgets. We had some great times together on a yacht before the war."[20]

Like Gatsby showing Nick Carraway his medal from Montenegro, Denny took photograph albums from a cabinet and paged through them with Michael. Michael was awestruck as he looked at the photographs of Denny in his white swimming trunks, standing with Prince Paul "upon some swaying Aegean deck."[21]

The phonograph records ran down. The photograph albums were put aside as the first light of dawn appeared behind the worn draperies. "The whisper of summer rain upon the gravel courtyard below lulled me to sleep, Denham's mouth, an artificial flower, crushed against my shoulder."[22]

The two slept through the day and were awakened in the evening by Denham's maid bringing in a tray with breakfast and the *Herald Tribune*.

"I detest the morning," Denny said as he drank calvados

and offered Michael coffee. "Call me sometime."

Michael finished his breakfast, dressed, and said goodbye.

Denny said nothing; he was studying the financial pages of the *Tribune*.

Michael was under his spell, riding the wave of a dopamine rush. "When I reached my hotel," Michael remembered, "I knew that the only place in the world I wanted to be was in Denham's bedroom."[23]

The next day, Michael moved in a haze. He couldn't paint. He walked through his favorite museums and "everything looked dull."[24] He couldn't concentrate. He couldn't sleep. More than anything, he wanted to call Denny, but was terrified to dial the telephone, paralyzed each time he looked at it.

Three days later, he reached a breaking point, picked up the telephone, and, around midnight, trembling, dialed Denny's number.

"Come over this time tomorrow," Denny responded.

The next day, Michael bought a violet satin tie and made cufflinks with golden bells on them that tinkled when he moved, to project, he hoped, an air of maturity beyond his years.

Michael couldn't help himself—he arrived early, before the appointed midnight hour. It was a mistake: Denny hadn't yet started the drinking that eased his transition from his opium dreams. He took one critical look at Michael, head to toe, and shook his head.

"Take off that God awful tie and unbutton your shirt down to your navel for Christ's sake" was how he greeted the infatuated teenager who had been desperate to detect some small sign of reciprocation of his love. Devastated, Michael wept.[25]

After ten years of effortlessly charming some of the richest, most celebrated men in the world, it was clear that

Denny could appear to others as something beyond the species "man," as a god, and was treated accordingly, pampered and spoiled; but all the worship could become wearisome when, despite his reputation and the legend growing around him, most of the time he felt like a mere mortal, if not a fraud, uncertain as to what inspired such other-worldly adoration. Whatever the inspiration, Denny had become dependent on this devotion for his sense of self worth.

In a little while, after bathing and putting on a white silk kimono that helped him get into character, Denham was himself again, wrestling with Trotsky on the bed, then bringing out and smoking jeweled opium pipes, offering each to Michael, beginning to talk with his young guest.

He told Michael how he had had a face peel to look younger, ten years younger by his own estimation, but "I couldn't go outdoors even in a light breeze without my face [becoming] one big bruise."[26]

Denny drew back the drapes and gazed at the night sky. "I love the stars today," he said, describing to Michael how they reminded him of the first time he had had sex, in Jacksonville, Florida. "Under the stars. That's where I screwed my beautiful brother. Oh boy! Was he beautiful. I never had it so good."[27]

Peter rationalized the affair Denny had begun with Michael, not surprised that Denny at thirty-two was living with a seventeen-year-old. Peter knew that "sexually he always liked and still likes boys about 14-16, which I could never understand and which horrifies me now. . ."[28] Peter had always been for him, he believed, "the responsible parent,"[29] and as the responsible parent, Peter was appalled that Denny, upon his return to Paris, immediately lapsed into his old ways, that his drug dependence and bizarre life, of staying out at the clubs all night, of returning in the morning with strangers, of not awakening until dark when the cycle would begin again, was ruining his life. Peter had tried every method to persuade

Denny to seek help for his addiction, to go to a detoxification clinic. "I have implored him to do something, appealed to his conscience, my wishes, everything, have done every [thing] except stop him from having money, as my god, I do really believe in freedom and free decision. I am racked by wondering what I could have done that I didn't do."[30] After a month of living with Denny, Peter couldn't take any more and was quite happy to leave the apartment to Denny and Michael, and spend the rest of the summer in Cannes.

Michael, too, knew Denny's lifestyle was self destructive, that his life was a form of escape, a slow suicide, perhaps "mocking the threat of maturity,"[31] and that "by addicting me to opium had imprisoned me within his dangerous life."[32] Michael was haunted by his fear of addiction, by his continuing questions about his sexuality, by his horror that he was frittering away his talents as an artist. He stumbled through his dream-like love-drugged days with Denny, sometimes not even aware if it was day or night. It made no difference. "I loved him so much that I only wanted to die in his shadow."[33]

There was no doubt about it, Denny could be as addictive as opium. When he had gauged well his anesthetic dosages, he was that rare individual who drew others into his orbit, who raised the sun and the moon and the stars for them whenever they were with him. Intelligent, humorous, charming, he made whoever he was with feel as if they were the center of his universe. For those with Denny, everyday was a special day, a holiday, a day of wonder. Michael followed Denny "willingly along the glassy arcades which led us to a lazy playground of waking dreams. I grew to adore nights, weeks, even months with him in that synthetic Eden, where there was no Eve, nor yet the viper with its entourage of judges, cruel school-teachers, pimps, interfering neighbors, disapproving parents, loveless clerics . . ."[34] In reflecting on Denny, Michael commented that "like all gigolos, and perhaps chameleons, he simply longed to please, which is to say to do his job well."[35]

Sleeping by day, the pair frequented the clubs and bars in the Bastille quarter by night. Denny would dress up—in an American sailor's suit, or white tie and tailcoat, or sometimes, when he didn't feel like dressing, in blue silk pajamas. Seeing Denny in what appeared to be costume, a patron of one of the clubs asked him at which theater he was performing. "La Vie" was his reply.[36]

Lying down on banquette in clubs, he fell asleep on so many occasions that he became known as "The Beautiful Sleeping Beauty." Michael roused him once, telling him he couldn't do that in a public place.

"Since you have turned my bedroom into a nightclub," Denny responded, "I don't see why I shouldn't turn your nightclub into a bedroom."[37]

From one imperious waiter who made it clear that he was not appreciative of Denny's style, Denny ordered "a glass of sperm."[38]

All nights ended in Denny's bedroom. Denny kissed Michael's throat: "From now on, baby, my heart murmurs only for you."[39] Michael again and again kissed "the scorpion tattooed in his groin."[40] In his diary, the love-struck teenager, so high on Denny, wrote: "Tonight the nearness of the remotest star taught me the possibility of *everything*."[41]

Michael may have felt he was living in Eden, but it was an Eden with at least one additional inhabitant. Each weekend, the two were joined by Denny's lover, Gerard, a sixteen-year-old boy he had met on a beach in Brittany. Gerard, with "his fresh salty skin," as Michael described him, "damp mouth and cumulus clouds of black curls tumbling into his wide, violet, conqueror's eyes,"[42] Gerard who, Denny believed—and this is what first attracted him to the teenager—had a body identical to his own, Gerard, a fisherman's son, adapted easily to this strange new world, dressing up in the suits Peter had bought for Denny, which were handmade by the tailor who worked for the Duke of Windsor, getting high on the cocaine Denny gave him, learning to flick open a Fabergé cigarette case with all the aplomb of a gentleman.

There were times Michael wasn't sure if he was in love with Denny, with Gerard, or both. One afternoon, while Denny slept, he took Gerard swimming at the Bains de Ligny on the Seine. When Denny learned how the two teenagers had spent the afternoon, he exploded: "That place is for boy-whores and people who like boy-whores," he shouted at Michael, "and since you are both it's no wonder that you go there. But it's not for Gerard, who is so innocent!"[43]

Peter returned to Paris in November to check on Denny and found that nothing had changed at 44 Rue du Bac while he was away, and now, for the first time, the landlord was pressing him to get Denny out of the apartment; the other residents of the building were complaining about him—the late night noise from the apartment, the obvious use of drugs, teenage boys who came and went at all hours. Peter ran away from the problem, going to New York City for the winter, hoping the landlord would put pressure on Denny and force him out of the apartment, saving him from the confrontation he dreaded.

Gerard was not the only crack in Michael's Eden. One evening, Michael entertained Jean Connolly, Cyril's wife, taking her to some of the clubs, finding her to be, as did Denny, "wonderful company, especially during the first stops on our endlessly exploitative club crawls,"[44] and then returning to 44 Rue du Bac at dawn so that she could visit with Denny. There they found Denny lying naked on the bathroom floor, "a hypodermic syringe hanging from his bleeding arm like a picador's dart from a bull's neck."[45] This was the first time Michael realized that his idol was using heroin. Afraid to summon help, Michael and Jean, quite drunk themselves, began pouring glasses of cold water over Denny, who at last came to, none the worse for wear. He dressed and shared a drink with them before she left.

Now even Denny seemed to realize that his life and drug habit were out of control. What was it all about? Who was he? How had this life ever happened? As the object of others' desire, he was an image, a fantasy that wasn't him but merely a reflection, someone they thought they saw. To others, he was everything. To him, they hardly existed. They wanted him, they wanted to be with him, they wanted to be him. Why, he wondered. Why? Why would anyone want to be me? What was it that made him so desirable? What they thought they saw today, would they still see tomorrow? The next day? Would he still embody their dreams next week? Although he looked like one, he knew he wasn't a god. Exactly what was it others were seeing? Had he become the reflection or was he still himself? Who was that?

CHAPTER TWO

"HOW DOES ONE MANAGE TO GET KEPT?"

How had it all begun?

There are just two glimpses of Denny's childhood growing up in Jacksonville, Florida, but both especially revealing.

Deeply moved by an article he had read in *Time* magazine about a German film director who had killed two horses to capture their death on film, Denny wrote a letter to *Time* which appeared in the June 21, 1926 issue:

> Sirs:
> I am but twelve years old, but I always have, and always will, detest any being (or fiend, as Subscriber Marlborough put the German, Schwarz) who would for the sake of anything, make life miserable for any dumb beast or animal. When I read the article on "Horses" [TIME, May 31, GERMANY] where the German moving picture producer, Schwarz, sprung a trap under two horses to make them tumble down the cliff onto the rocks below for the sake of making moving pictures of their agony, I felt as one would if someone would suddenly tell you that a certain man had tortured every baby in the world to his death. I

felt like writing to TIME and telling to TIME how I felt, but I said to myself "TIME has no place for little boys" and I dropped the subject, but when I read the letter of Karl Busch [TIME, June 7, LETTERS] [Busch had opined in his letter that Americans seemed "unable to appreciate the artistic honesty of director Schwarz"] I could not restrain. I say "Let Busch have his own opinion, everyone has, but it is my opinion that not many will agree with Mr. Busch.

DENHAM FOUTS

Jacksonville, Fla.

For a twelve-year-old boy to be reading *Time* in 1926 was remarkable enough; for that twelve year old to be moved to compose and send a letter of that maturity says so much, both about Denny's intelligence and about his compassion. The boy who felt so strongly about two horses being killed for the benefit of a film is the same man walking along a Santa Monica beach eighteen years later in December of 1944, where happening upon a seagull with a broken wing, he amputated the wing to make the bird more comfortable.

The other glimpse of his boyhood is just as revealing. Denny was raised in a family of moderate means but imbued with the old Southern aristocratic tradition, with all that implied about adherence to custom, traditions, conservative thought. Denny's paternal grandfather was vice president of a railroad, his maternal grandfather founded the Atlantic National Bank and the Timuquana County Club. Denny's father, Edwin Louis Fouts, graduated from Yale in 1910, worked in his father-in-law's bank in Boca Grande, then moved the family to Jacksonville where he was employed at the Florida Broom Company and later started Fouts

18

Manufacturing, an asbestos awning business, but never quite measuring up to his father's high expectations for him.

Denny's love of thumbing his nose at tradition, of doing whatever he pleased, surfaced in his teenage years. An essay he wrote for his school newspaper, a strident defense of socialism, may well have been the least of the infractions which got this teenager—who had "screwed my beautiful brother" outdoors under the stars—expelled from high school. This was not the sort of son parents would want to have around their daughter, Ellen, a year younger than Denny, and their son, Frederic, four years younger than Denny, if alternatives were available. Denny's father asked his uncle, who was president of Safeway Supermarket Stores, to find a job for his wayward son in Washington, D.C.

Not much more was happening in Washington in 1933 for an intelligent, restless, hormonally supercharged nineteen year old than in Jacksonville, and after a few months Denny had made his way to Manhattan, found a job in those bleak Depression days as a General Foods stock boy bagging groceries and wrapping packages, and shared a small apartment with an acquaintance.

It was there, in New York City, that Denny first awakened to his extraordinary powers. He experienced the surprise, then intoxication, of having all heads turn his way whenever he walked into Jimmie Daniels nightclub in Harlem, one of his favorite haunts. Walking along a city street, people stopped and stared. Wherever he went, everyone was gazing at him, watching him, listening to whatever he said, flattering him, fussing over him, following him, doting on him. Even though he had achieved nothing, he commanded every room he entered. Everyone seemed flustered when first introduced to him and looked at him with an intensity both frightening and affirming. And after those first long looks he would begin receiving invitations to bars, to dinners, to Broadway shows, to opening night parties, personal tours of museums, weekends at vacation homes, trips to Europe. Wherever he was taken, he was always treated. A heady experience for a teenager from the sticks who had known only rejection, of being expelled from school, thrown out by his family, who had the most menial job, no higher education, no family connections. Suddenly, artists, musicians, actors, producers, executives, diplomats, royalty, were his friends. Suddenly, for no apparent reason, for nothing he had done or said, he was the center of attention, center stage. And loving it.

Perhaps everyone is born with some certain gift. It may be the ability to pitch a ball, to carry a tune, it may be a feel for numbers, a gift of persuasion. Some may sense early on, intuitively, what their gift is, others may spend a lifetime trying to find it. Denny was bright enough to begin putting the pieces together: he realized he was blessed with a special magnetism, that his appearance drew people to him so that they enjoyed talking with him and being with him and buying him whatever he wanted.

How could he capitalize on this unique gift? How could he cooperate in whatever fantasy people saw in him that gave him such power over them? Could he become the embodiment of their desire? Was there a way to find a wealthy patron, someone who would worship him and see it as their mission to take care of him, and not only take care of him, but to support him in the style he was encountering as he moved around the highest reaches of New York society? Denny had no interest in being a hustler. By the way so many people were responding to his looks, to his love potion that drew them to him, he knew instinctively that he had what it took to be well kept. And he very quickly was becoming partial to all the best money could buy. But how did one go about finding a proper celebrant—benefactor?

Through his roommate who worked in a Manhattan bookstore, Denny met best-selling author Glenway Wescott who frequented the shop. Thirty-three-year-old Wescott, who had traveled widely and been part of the young generation of expatriates living in Europe after the First World War, knew just about every poet, writer and artist of his day, and at that time, for winning the prestigious Harper Prize with the publication in 1927 of his novel *The Grandmother*, was himself as famous as Ernest Hemingway and F. Scott Fitzgerald. He projected a worldliness and the understanding of an older friend who could look deep into Denny's soul and know just what he was thinking. Denny had snagged his first celebrity and found his first mentor.

It was the spring of 1934. Denny, Wescott remembered, "would call on me—I was living on Murray Hill—whenever he was hungry or felt like asking questions about how to get on in the world, which I would answer, all purely Socratic."[1]

Wescott warmed to the topic and this Socratic dialogue went on for a number of sessions.

"Now, Glenway," Denny would say in his deep seductive Southern drawl, "you know everything. I want you to tell me: how does one manage to get kept?"

Wescott found his naiveté amusing. He laughed.

"To begin with," he explained to his attentive student, "you must never use that word—'kept.' Think of something you want to do that takes money to learn. Then ask someone for help and guidance. You'll get much more money that way than by coming at it straight on."[2]

Denny was a quick study. He was perfecting the art of opening doors with his looks, and, with his charm and intelligence, was mingling easily with the city's upper crust. It wasn't long before the handsome, suddenly sophisticated twenty year old from a middle-class background in Jacksonville was accompanying a German baron to Europe.

Denny still had much to learn. In Berlin, he and the baron fought, Denny packed and started hitchhiking to Venice. On his way, the chauffeured limousine of an old Greek shipping magnate pulled over, picked him up, and headed on to Venice where they boarded the tycoon's yacht. Again Denny hadn't yet mastered all the rules of engagement and fell in love with one of the sailors on the yacht. After the two of them stole as much money as they could, several thousand dollars, they jumped ship and took a suite at the Quisisana Hotel on Capri. The sailor left when the money ran out, while Denny continued each evening to dress for dinner in his new formal wear, hoping to be seen. When at last it became apparent that he could not pay his bills at the Quisisana, the police were summoned and Denny was escorted through the lobby.

It was at that very moment that Evan Morgan, the last Lord Tredegar, walking through the lobby with his wife, trailed by a retinue of retainers, spotted Denny and commanded the authorities: "Unhand that handsome youth, he is mine."[3]

CHAPTER THREE

"MY DEAR DENHAM"

Evan Morgan was the only son of the third Lord Tredegar - Courtenay Morgan—and of the Lady Katherine Agnes Blanche Carnegie. The old Tredegar family fortune in coal funded a 121,000 acre estate in Monmouthshire in south Wales, as well as property along entire city streets in London. Their sprawling seventeenth century country house was one of the most magnificent in Great Britain, with its paneled rooms, windows framed by heavy velvet draperies, state rooms lit by hundreds of candles casting light and shadows on coats of arms, massive gold-framed family portraits, and elaborate molded ceilings inset with oval paintings. Tredegar House was run by a staff of forty-five servants who lived and worked in the mansion, with more in charge of the grounds, the brewery, the bakery, the gardens. There were housemaids, groomsmen, an indoor gardener, a hall boy, stickmen to provide wood for the many fireplaces, housekeepers, coachmen, valets, footmen, a lodge keeper, bricklayer, stone mason, scullery maid, deer keeper, kennel keeper—a small army of servants, some of whom were the third and fourth generations to live and work on the estate.

Evan's father passed his time in the usual pursuits of the landed gentry—hunting, shooting, fishing, and sailing his steam yacht, *Liberty*, one of the largest private yachts afloat.

He was proficient at each pastime, but his real goal was in getting away from Tredegar House as frequently as possible, for Lady Katherine had severe mental problems and had come to believe she was a bird and had built for herself a large nest in one of the mansion's sitting rooms, and there she sat, wearing a cloth beak.

What chance would a boy have growing up in this home? Evan quite predictably was quite an eccentric. "Evan's misfortune," one friend said, "was to have been born with far too much money ... and no practical sense at all."[1]

Evan, who fancied himself a poet, mingled with the authors and artists of the day, some of whom painted vivid word portraits of their wealthy acquaintance. Poet and author Nancy Cunard called Evan "a fantasy who could be most charming and most bitchy."[2] Aldous Huxley reported to a friend that "I like him, I think, quite a lot, tho' he is the most fearfully spoilt child."[3] Going for a walk during a visit at Garsington in November of 1917, Virginia Woolf encountered a car "full of speckled and not prepossessing young men ...The most obvious was Evan Morgan, a little red absurdity, with a beak of a nose, no chin, and a general likeness to a very callow but student Bantam cock, who has run to legs & neck. However, he was evidently most carefully prepared to be a poet & an eccentricity, both by his conversation, which aimed at irresponsible brilliance, & lack of reticence, & by his clothes, which must have been copied from the usual Shelley picture. But he was as innocent as a chicken & so foolish it didn't seem to matter."[4] An acquaintance described him as being "tall and very thin, with odd articulated movements, as if preparing to spread wings in flight."[5] His voice "had a lilt to it, and his speech was often broken by a snort as he took another pinch of snuff. He appeared utterly confident, utterly relaxed ...but very evidently a man of vivid caprice . . ."[6] Evan at the time served as the unpaid secretary to the Parliamentary secretary of the Ministry of Labour.

24

It was in London at the Restaurant de la Tour Eiffel on Percy Street off Tottenham Court Road, a restaurant popular both with the aristocracy and the artistic set, that Evan met with this coterie of poets, painters, authors, actors, and musicians—Duff Cooper, Nancy Cunard, Wyndham Lewis, Michael Arlen, George Bernard Shaw, Igor Stravinsky, Augustus John, Aldous Huxley, Dylan Thomas, the Sitwells. Cheerleader and instigator of this group dubbed by the press the "Bright Young People," Evan, never one to tolerate boredom, devised adventures such as a midnight treasure hunt in London in which the participants had a list of objects to find and bring to a two a.m. party, or dinners to which the guests came dressed as young children and acted accordingly.[7] A young man at one of Evan's events remembered how it "began at the Eiffel Tower [restaurant] and ended at somebody's bedroom at Prince's Hotel in Jermyn Street" and how, at that point, he left abruptly "clutching my remaining bits of virtue—bundled them into a taxi and trundled home. I've never seen anything so stupendously naughty, even in Oxford! Never again—as I value my reputation."[8]

In a moment of clarity, Evan's mother, worried about her son, offered to pay all expenses for Aldous Huxley, then teaching at Eton, to chaperone him on a trip abroad, hoping, as Huxley put it, "that my respectable middle-aged temperament would act as a slight brake to Evan's whirligig habits." The inability to get a wartime passport prevented their travels, but Huxley witnessed an example of these "whirligig habits" the very next day while at the studio of an artist "spasmodically trying to paint a nude study from a very lovely little model with red hair ... Evan and the model became increasingly affectionate."[9]

One of the Bright Young People, the popular novelist Ronald Firbank, had set his sights on Evan, who had filled out a little since Virginia Woolf had viewed him as a "student Bantam cock," doe-eyed Evan with his wavy light brown hair and sensuous lips. Evan at first was fascinated by his conversations with the older Firbank, conversations, as he characterized them, "of a most speculative and dubious character,"[10] conversations that made Evan feel that his admirer was "under the influence of Bacchus ... at least you could never tell because his conversation was equally wild either way."[11] One friend noted Ronald "Firbank spoke only in strangled and disjointed gasps of rapture, hilarity and dismay."[12] He wore, Evan observed, shirts of a color "never seen off the stage" and his ties were "very bohemian."[13] But it was his hands that most troubled Evan, those well groomed nails with a deep carmine polish, those hands, one could never tell where they might "find themselves."[14]

Evan was amused by Firbank and viewed him "as one might some rare bird to be cherished for its exquisite exotic qualities rather than as a human being,"[15] but his amusement began to turn to concern when he realized that Firbank was cherishing him in a very different way (Firbank's nickname for Evan was "Heaven Organ"),[16] and those troublesome hands kept finding themselves in the wrong places.

Twenty-seven-year-old Evan dutifully told his father that his relationship with Firbank was becoming of "deep concern" to him, and noted how Firbank had a habit of "running his fingers through his hair, 'just like a woman, my dear'" leading to some "sinister suspicions concerning him."[17] Firbank proudly had told Evan of his plan to dedicate to him his latest novel, *The Princess Zouburoff*, with a dedication that would read: "To the Hon. Evan Morgan in Souvenir Amicale of a 'Previous Incarnation.'"[18] (When Firbank first met Evan, he told him that his profile was identical to that of the mummy of Ramses, and that he must be a reincarnation of the ancient Egyptian pharaoh.) This was a little much, especially since Evan was finding himself attracted not to Firbank but to another member of his coterie, the composer Philip Heseltine, a friend from his Eton and Oxford days. Aghast at Firbank's proposed dedication, Evan had his father instruct the family solicitors to intercede and communicate to Firbank that should his new book ever be published with that dedication, Evan Morgan would "take such steps as he may be advised to protect his interest and to make his views on the subject perfectly clear to the public and his friends."[19] The publisher had the dedication page physically cut from each book before it was released.

Other fathers were warning their sons about Evan, just as Lord Tredegar cautioned Evan about Firbank. While a student at Eton, Alan Pryce-Jones' father had taken him aside in his library and said, "You are old enough to know that there exists a man named Evan Morgan. He is a first cousin of your friend Pinhead. And I tell you here and now that should you ever find yourself in the same room, you are to leave immediately."[20] "Why?" Alan innocently asked his father, who responded that "he would tell me one day ... one day when I was older." Ominous words, to be sure, and words that Alan's father never elaborated upon; and of course Alan's response was to pester Pinhead immediately to introduce him to Evan Morgan. Pinhead did—"we took to one another at once"—and they became friends. "I had no reason to be other than grateful to him for as much affection as his leprechaun character would bestow on a friend."[21] Another young man worried about a *Vogue* portrait that showed him standing next to Evan Morgan: "The ravishing beauty of my face and my figure rendered my proximity to this old starfish most suspicious to the ignorant."[22]

It had not been so many years before that Oscar Wilde had been sentenced to two years of hard labor in Reading Gaol for the attraction he felt toward Bosie, Lord Alfred Douglas. Evan, a good friend of Lord Alfred, whom he considered "the greatest sonneteer since Shakespeare,"[23] was very much aware of this when he contemplated Ronald Firbank's feelings toward him, and his own toward Philip Heseltine.

It was just at this point in his life that Evan took up the notion of becoming a priest, and became the first Tredegar in five centuries to join the Roman Catholic Church. After he had one of the family's Rolls Royces fitted with an altar, his chauffeur drove him to Rome where he entered the Vatican seminary. Perhaps it was because he sent his valet to attend all his classes and take notes that he never did become a priest, but certainly all was not lost. In 1923, at the age of thirty, he was made the Privy Chamberlain of the Sword and Cape by Pope Benedict XV (and continued in the same office under Pope Pius XI), an office that entitled him to flamboyant robes, which he wore for his formal portrait that hung at Tredegar House, and that, in fact, he wore whenever possible. His friend Nancy Cunard remembered seeing Evan in Rome dressed as "some sort of papal chamberlain," wearing something that to her resembled "a British admiral's uniform—the hat particularly."[24] Another friend described him as "an 18th century figure come to life again."[25] And later Gore Vidal recalled seeing him carrying "a big attaché case with the Tredegar coat of arms, more elaborate than the Queen of England's."[26] Evan's religious convictions were erratic at best. He once owned a relic of the true Cross, but mislaid it in an all male Turkish bath.

Evan was ordered by his father to marry and produce an heir after Evan's sister, Gwyneth, had drowned in the Thames—a drug related suicide, it was rumored. Ideas of the priesthood abandoned, Evan, in 1928, married Lois Sturt (a "most unwilling bride" one friend observed),[27] the strikingly beautiful daughter of the 2nd Baron Alington and Lady Feodorowna Yorke. As Gore Vidal further noted, this "glamorous Mountbatten world" was "boldly bisexual. Bloomsbury with coronets. And everybody got married."[28] Lois had been a film star in the early 1920s and had been the lover of the 15th Earl of Pembroke and of Prince George, the duke of Kent, soon to become King George VI of England.

Prince George had wanted to marry her, but the royal family opposed the union due to her "fast" reputation.

It was on the world travels of this couple—who were often, as a friend commented in "remote communication"[29]— that Evan happened to spot Denham Fouts in the lobby of the Quisisana Hotel on Capri.

Was Evan's wife concerned when her husband so suddenly made a new friend who was now part of their entourage as they continued the Grand Tour, or did she consider this just another manifestation of Evan's charming eccentricities, another addition to his unusual collection of acquaintances? In China, they visited the opium dens where Denny sampled the wares and developed an addiction.

When Evan's father died, Evan became Lord Tredegar, a viscount and baron, lord of 500-year-old Tredegar House. And then the fun began.

The glitterati, along with the beautiful and the handsome unknowns, made their way to his infamous weekend garden parties at Tredegar Park: H.G. Wells, Marchesa Casati, Aleister Crowley, Lord Alfred Douglas, Lady Nancy Cunard, the painter Augustus John, George Bernard Shaw, William Butler Yeats, G.K. Chesterton, Aldous Huxley. Denny was right at home in this glamorous party world and became a part of it: from Jacksonville, Florida, to one of the grandest manors of the English-speaking world.

In addition to the menagerie of guests, Evan had assembled at his estate a menagerie of animals. There was Somerset, the boxing kangaroo with which Evan invariably boxed a few rounds at each party, Alice the honey bear, Blue Boy, a rather frightening macaw that perched on Evan's shoulder spitting out obscenities and that seemed to have a particular dislike for H.G. Wells, attacking the famed author with hammer-like blows. There were also baboons that stalked and terrified the hapless gardeners, as well as anteaters, pigeons, birds of prey, falcons and owls that Evan trained to swoop over the guests. He would call "Rosa, Rosa" and Rosa, a duck, would fly straight to him from the other side of the lake in the park; as a friend noted, "Birds came crowding round him like spinsters round a popular preacher."[30] To the delight of his guests, he had trained Blue Boy to climb up his leg inside his trousers and push its beak out through his fly.[31]

Drink and drugs fueled these circus-like gatherings. "He's one of the very few people I know who *can* throw a party," one of the guests, Aleister Crowley, recorded with admiration in his diary.[32] Another guest, the socialite Sir Henry "Chips" Channon, MP, wrote in his diary that Tredegar House had "the feel and even smell of decay, of aristocracy in extremis, the sinister and the trivial, crucifixes and crocodiles..."[33]

Among the guests at Evan's weekend parties was Crown Prince Paul of Greece, living in exile in England since 1924 when the Greek Assembly had abolished the monarchy and declared Greece a republic. From that time, members of the royal family were forbidden to live in Greece, and twenty-three-year-old Paul and his older brother, King George II, had sought refuge in London. Paul, an athletic man, tall, broad-shouldered, with a jovial laugh and ready smile, on a lark had assumed an alias and found a job in a London factory constructing airplanes, though most of his time was spent moving in the upper social circles. And one weekend, at a party at Tredegar House, the Prince met Denham Fouts.

As captivated by Denny as was Lord Tredegar, Prince Paul took Denny with him on a cruise around the Mediterranean. "We had some great times together on a yacht," Denny always would remember as he took out photograph albums to show his friends. And there he was, looking "very glamorous in belted white swimming trunks, leaning with merited narcissism against a lifebelt, upon some swaying Aegean deck."[34]

Back in Jacksonville, Florida, Denny's mother worried

about her son. According to one of Denny's cousins, "he sent continual postcards from all over the world. Sometimes he would send photos of him with a glamorous woman or a handsome man: 'Traveling here with Lady So-and-So in Malay. She thinks she's Marlene Dietrich and so do I.' But he never would give anybody an address to write back."[35]

CHAPTER FOUR

"A KNIGHT IN SHINING ARMOR"

A baron. A shipping tycoon. A lord. A prince. Denny had mastered Glenway Wescott's lessons very well indeed, and was prepared for his next conquest.

To be young, handsome, bright, and rich were the blessings bestowed upon Peter Watson, and he wore those blessings lightly, with grace and style. He was the youngest child of Sir George Watson, Lord of the Manor of Sulhamstead Abbotts, who had invented margarine and made a fortune when butter was rationed in Great Britain during the First World War. Peter was educated at Eton and Oxford and studied in Munich where his interest in modern art awakened and where he purchased his first Picasso drawing. When his father died in 1930, Peter at twenty-two was the beneficiary of trusts, which gave him the wealth to be a gentleman of leisure and to pursue his passion for art. The world became his playground—letters written on stationery of the finest hotels, postcards from the best resorts, spewed forth to his friends, and if, for instance, it happened to be raining when he was in Salzburg, he simply packed up and headed off to Venice. Everyone who became his friend considered themselves fortunate. Alan Pryce-Jones, a classmate from his Eton days, described Peter as "slow-speaking, irresistibly beguiling

...from fourteen or so onwards, one of the most sophisticated beings I ever knew: rich, funny, and wise . . ."[1] Cecil Beaton found that Peter's "wry sense of humor and mysterious qualities of charm made him unlike anyone I had known,"[2] that he was "an independent, courageous person, on terms of absolute honesty with himself, with the world and with everybody he talks to."[3] The poet Stephen Spender thought Peter "quite unsnobbish, completely generous, quite unvulgar."[4] Spender recalled his first encounters with Peter: "When I think of him then, I think of his clothes, which were beautiful, his general neatness and cleanness, which seemed almost those of a handsome young Bostonian, his Bentley and his chauffeur who had been the chauffeur of the Prince of Wales, one wonderful meal we had in some village of the Savoie, and his knowing that the best food in Switzerland is often to be found at the buffets of railway stations."[5]

Peter was tall, imperially slim, debonair, with a smile that "was so disarming that people could not but like him," as Cecil Beaton described it.[6] Beaton called him "the best person at the art of living I know."[7] He was, in Beaton's judgment, "a completely fulfilled, integrated person; someone who has been through many vicissitudes and has now discovered himself."[8] Beaton also described Peter's thick brown hair as being "sexily lotioned" with brilliantine,[9] a choice of words that pretty much summed up the problem: Peter was so perfect that woman, and men, kept weaving their fantasies around him and falling in love with him. And Beaton, who would become the famed society photographer, fell very hard indeed.

Beaton knew exactly the moment it happened. It was late summer, 1930. Cecil was twenty-six, four years older than Peter. They were in Vienna, each with his own friends, when they met. Peter went with Cecil to antique shops to help him select furnishings for Ashcombe, his new country estate. Cecil could not understand why his friends were making such a fuss about this young man until several days later, as they went down on the same elevator from their hotel rooms, "he shot me a glance of sympathy, of amusement—it may have been a wink—but it did its work—it went straight to my heart—and from that moment I was hypnotized by him: watching every gesture of his heavy hands, the casual languid way he walked."[10] As they got out of the elevator, "we burst into laughter, and arm-in-arm walked off into the Vienna side-streets to become the greatest of friends."[11]

Cecil was a man obsessed. He began molding himself to be just like Peter, buying the same clothes, using the same cologne, combing his hair the same way, imitating his walk, the way he talked—to the extent that Cecil's family could not distinguish Cecil from Peter on the telephone. Hoping that he could make Peter fall in love with him, he invited Peter to join him on a tour of the southern United States, of the Bahamas, Haiti, Havana, Vera Cruz, Mexico City, and Honolulu. Peter, who in spite of his wealth had never been abroad, thought it might be fun.

It was quite a voyage across on the *Aquitania* that January of 1931. As Cecil wrote in his diary: "My eyes were glued to him throughout the day and as he lay asleep. The sea air knocked him out most of the time and as he lay, big hands clasped on his chest with his head thrown to the side, I would get out a sketching book and make drawings of him. It was the most heavenly experience in the world to live here in this cabin with him, to dress together in the morning and evening, to play the gramophone ... to have baths together."[12] Peter seemed unaware of the longing eyes locked upon him until the moment Cecil made the mistake of giving words to his fantasy and saying to Peter, "One day when we are lovers ..."[13] Cecil instantly knew from Peter's annoyance that the object of his desire did not feel the same way about him. Cecil already had arranged for an enormous bouquet of lillies-of-the-valley and violets to be delivered to Peter when they landed in New York City, to be accompanied with a note: "To Peter who I love so much."[14] The arrival of the flowers led to Peter initiating a frank conversation about the nature and boundaries of their friendship, though this discussion did little to cool Cecil's infatuation. For the remainder of the trip Cecil played the role of friend, while internally going through soaring highs and plunging lows, times when Peter's "dirty handkerchiefs, his every belonging possessed a glamour," and other times when he concluded that Peter was "independent, selfish, rude, insolent, conceited, young and silly and completely unimportant."[15]

Peter certainly didn't make it any easier for Cecil and seemed oblivious to the powers he held over his traveling companion. Often on their journey they slept in the same bed. As Beaton confided to his diary: "How we gossiped. We giggled ...We fought gaily in bed, completely upsetting the bedclothes. We tickled each other, lay in one another's arms and I was completely happy—as completely as I ever will be with this poppet because he is the most unperturbed bastard, uninfluencible and I shall never alas become his lover."[16] This realization could not stop Cecil from spending "half the night looking lovingly and longingly at him in his poses of profound unconsciousness. I loved his big fat veiny hands and would clasp them around me in his sleep."[17]

Truman Capote knew both Watson and Beaton. He and Cecil were lifelong friends, but Capote was one of the very few who had no use for Peter. Capote felt Watson had a sadistic streak, and brutally portrayed this voyage abroad the *Aquitania* in "Unspoiled Monsters," a chapter of his never-completed, long-anticipated novel, *Answered Prayers*. "Once," Capote wrote in a parenthetical remark in this chapter, "Watson deliberately set forth on a sea voyage halfway round the world with an aristocratic, love-besotted young man whom he punished by never permitting a kiss or caress, though night after night they slept in the same narrow bed—that is, Mr. Watson slept while his perfectly decent but disintegrating friend twitched with insomnia and an aching scrotum."[18]

Back in London, Cecil time and again would resign himself to their being no more than "affectionate companions,"[19] though each time Peter would call him to go horseback riding, to visit an antique shop or gallery, to play backgammon, Cecil once again fell under his spell, convinced anew he could win his love, only to discover anew each time that he could not. The emotional turmoil was too much for him and through hypnosis he sought a cure for his addiction to Peter, a procedure that brought only temporary relief. While going on with his work and his life, he waited for the telephone to ring, for Peter to call. When he was ill, he attributed his illness to not having seen Peter for too long a time. When a friend told him Peter had asked about him, he was ecstatic and wrote in his diary: "I now feel I would like to get physically well, my body in good trim, my tummy muscles tightened, my skin a different colour, my hair thicker and then go back to the friendship that has cost me so much happiness, but which on account of its disadvantages I was silly (?) strong (?) enough to relinquish."[20]

In May of 1935, Peter and Cecil both happened to be in Paris and made plans to meet for dinner, but Peter did not appear at the agreed upon time. Cecil later learned that Peter that night had met in a nightclub a young American named Denham Fouts.

As Peter recalled the moment: "He took me back to his hotel where he gave himself cocaine injections." And there, in Denny's hotel room, Peter stayed.[21]

Stephen Spender once noted that Peter's education "had all been through love: through love of beautiful works and through love of people in whom he saw beauty."[22] When Peter saw Denny in that Parisian nightclub, he had an instantaneous physical response to what he saw, as though he had discovered beauty itself, and he knew he had to possess this god-like creature as much as he had to possess the museum quality paintings of de Chirico, Gris, Klee, Miro, and Picasso he had been collecting. Denny may have found himself falling in love, though, more likely, he sensed he had found himself someone who might be a worthy acolyte; he played his hand and, as scheduled, a few days later left on a tramp steamer for New York. Peter was hooked.

Cecil was devastated when he learned of Peter's feelings for Denny, "again conscious of my failure," as he wrote in his diary, "that my beloved will never be in love with me and will always fall for strumpets, and that continuously I am going to be miserable through each intrigue."[23] He no longer could deal with this unrequited love, and drafted a letter to Peter:

> My dearest Darling, this is so much the saddest thing that happened in my life. It is so serious for me to make the painful wrench but I *cannot* continue being made miserably unhappy constantly by your peculiar vagaries ...I cannot weep any more, my eyes are swollen and my face unrecognizable from so many tears and so much hysteria.[24]

Cecil never mailed his letter, but read it to Peter, who tried to heal their friendship and urged that they remain "sane and friends again."[25]

Just as Cecil Beaton's life changed forever when he met Peter Watson—and, to the end of his life, even after many other affairs, including one with Greta Garbo, considered Peter "the love of his life" and still was "sad and sore that it was never a mutual love affair, a friendship only for him,"[26]— so Peter Watson's life was to change forever that evening he met Denham Fouts. A friend of both Peter and Denny would call Denny "the great, destructive, love" of Peter's life.[27] Denny well knew what he was doing in leaving for New York after he had aroused Peter's interest: Peter could not live without him. "We corresponded and he came back to live with me in London."[28]

Stephen Spender realized Peter "was too perfectionist to be an easy person to live with ... He was, as it were, essentially made for honeymoons and not for marriages. I mean that the best possible relationship to have with Peter was to be taken up by him very intensely for a few weeks, and then simply to remain on his visiting list for the rest of one's time."[29] When Denny returned to London, to Peter, the honeymoon began, a whirlwind fantasy Denny never could have imagined. Peter took him to all his favorite haunts in London, in Paris, Zurich, Cannes, Nice, Monte Carlo, St. Moritz, Milan, Florence, Rome, Capri, halcyon days visiting museums, galleries, sightseeing, bicycling, swimming, evenings at the best restaurants and nightclubs, plays, operas, on to China and the Far East.

As Stephen Spender so well recognized, this was the fun part of being with Peter, the magical part, and Denny must have felt the career Glenway Wescott had launched him on had reached its zenith. Thereafter, though the two became co-dependent, Peter's relationship with Denny never was easy. Denny, Peter came to understand, "had no confidence in anyone—this stimulated me and [I] thought if I took trouble he would in me."[30] Peter may have recognized something of himself in Denny. He once confessed to a friend that "without some money I would have acted worse than you. I can't do anything and I hate *doing* things."[31] And this recognition about himself may have led him to keep trying with Denny, to want to help him reach the potential he saw in him, to inspire him to do something more than sit around being beautiful, to make him realize his worth lay in more than his looks.

No matter how much beauty, self assurance, and confidence they project, those select few who look like a god may feel the same insecurities and self doubts as everyone else, sometimes even more if they are unsure, as was Denny, as to just what it was they possessed that drew another's attention or love. Exactly what was it that he could do with his life? What was his purpose? Denny, Peter discovered, was "terribly neurotic (his drawings are nightmares of frustrations and obscenities)."[32] Although only six years younger than Peter, Denny, at twenty-one, still looked like a teenager, and Peter, at twenty-seven, like an adult, and those in fact were the roles they assumed. "I became for him of course the responsible parent who just provided him with money."[33] As hard as Peter tried, he found, to his disappointment, that "we never shared any intellectual interests whatsoever and he always resented that side of me." And the sexual side of their relationship disappointed Peter, too. "Going to bed is a physical act with him, no more, he is stuck at 16 years old and resists any attempt to grow. And yet I feel it must be my fault, somehow."[34]

And yet, Peter could no more move beyond Denny, despite repeated sessions with German émigré psychiatrist Dr. Karl Bluth, than Cecil could get over Peter.

Cecil Beaton, of course, hated Denny with "an unconsumed passion," and when he heard through his friends of "the appalling dogfights that Denham had with Peter," he noted with delight in his diary that "they were just what Peter needed."[35]

The dogfights typically began with Peter's concern about Denny's opium habit, a habit that had begun when he joined the world tour with Lord Tredegar and his wife and with them visited the opium dens in China. Peter always had been frightened of drugs and was distressed at what he saw them doing to Denny. He tried every stratagem to get him to quit— love, reasoning, nagging, threats—nothing, of course, worked against the power of Denny's addiction. Every once in a while, Peter was able to get Denny into a rehabilitation clinic but those "cures" proved temporary, very temporary, at best. And so their fighting continued.

After such fights, when the two separated, Denny was never at a loss finding room and board. Peter learned later that Denny once had gone and "joined the Hitler Jugend in Germany and was a boy friend of Richtofen, the Nazi ace" with whom he attended Nazi rallies in Berlin.[36] Richtofen was Wolfram Freiherr von Richtofen, almost twenty years older than Denny, married, with three children and was the cousin of Manifred von Richtofen who was Germany's most famous ace, and is still today considered the ace of aces and a legend as the "Red Baron." Wolfram had served during the First World War and himself achieved the designation of flying ace for the number of enemy aircrafts he shot down; when Hermann Goering formed the Luftwaffe in 1933, he joined, and later became one of only six Luftwaffe officers to become a Field Marshall. It was during his stay in Germany with Richtofen that Denny met Adolf Hitler, which led to Truman Capote's conjecture, which he loved to repeat, that "had Denham Fouts yielded to Hitler's advances there would have been no World War Two."[37]

Other times after Peter and Denny fought, Denny would go back to Prince Paul, but now, with the national plebiscite in Greece in 1935 that had called for a return of the monarchy, Crown Prince Paul was no longer in London; he had joined his brother's triumphant return to Greece, and there, in Athens, obtained for Denny a suite of rooms in the Grande Bretagne Hotel.

Denny was well aware of the power he held there, even after Prince Paul on January 8, 1938 married Princess Frederica of Hanover, a great-great-granddaughter of Queen Victoria and the granddaughter of Kaiser Wilhelm II. In the bar in the Grande Bretagne Hotel, Denny in 1938 had met twenty-two-year-old surrealist artist Brion Gysin, whose acquaintances, including Salvador Dali, Pablo Picasso, Gertrude Stein, and Alice B. Toklas, all agreed he looked like a young Greek god, perhaps Apollo, maybe Dionysus or

Narcissus. Denny spotted this classically handsome young man sitting at the bar and took him up to his rooms. There, he picked up the telephone, called the front desk and asked to be put through to the Royal Palace. When Prince Paul was given the telephone, Denny asked that he immediately send over "one of those royal guards in ballet skirts with something for us to smoke." The Prince did, Denny and Brion did, and as Brion recalled, "we got royally stoned."[38]

Brion Gysin was fascinated by everything about Denny, from the suitcases that Salvador Dali had decorated for him with labels like "Hotel Sordide" and "Midnight Motel," to the expensive sports jackets Peter had brought for him, which appeared to be "itchy tweed but felt like cat's fur woven into cashmere."[39] For a while they enjoyed each other's company and together migrated back to Paris. The two were like brothers in their desire to live well, and in their ability, through the largesse of admirers, to live well without working.

In Paris, newlyweds Jane and Paul Bowles befriended Brion at a Left Bank Café, and Brion introduced them to Denny. One evening, Brion and Denny drove the Bowles to dinner and then to the premiere of Stravinsky's "Dumbarton Oaks Concerto." Bowles learned that Denny on his journeys with Peter had been to Tibet but could not determine what he had done there except for his story that he had been practicing archery and had brought back with him some large tribal bows. To show off the skills he had developed, Denny took an arrow, which had a built in tampon that he soaked in ether, lit it, aimed out the hotel window, and shot into the night traffic on the Champs-Elyées. Brion found this amusing, though Paul Bowles, who had no use for Denny, found this conduct astounding, and noted in his memoirs that "fortunately there were no repercussions."[40]

There are those whose personalities are so addicting that, for all their faults, life is richer, more fun, with them; without them, the world beats empty and hollow. Denny had this power to addict, and Peter, the addict, could not be separated for long from what he had to have. Denny had become addicted to being desired, and, in being the object of desire had found his self worth. The two needed each other and invariably reunited.

Although Peter said that he couldn't do anything and hated doing things, he had quietly become a forceful presence in London's art world. He orchestrated major art exhibitions that drew thousands of visitors, organized concerts, and behind the scenes helped many young artists. John Craxton, who became a prominent neo-Romantic artist, was, as a teenager, living in a small flat with his parents and six siblings, with no room to paint. He received a letter from Peter Watson, who had seen his work: "I have been reading an article by Miro called *'je reve d'un grand atelier,'* and it occurs to me that you must need a studio. Find one and send me the bill." Craxton came to consider Peter "a second father in a way, tremendously generous, a great catalyst and encourager."[41] Craxton set up a studio in Abercorn Place, which he then shared with another young artist, Lucien Freud, who would become a lionized British realist painter. Peter later paid for Craxton and Freud to visit Greece so that they could see more of the world than London. Peter in 1938 funded the publication costs of Charles Henri Ford's first book of poems, *The Garden of Disorder*, and repeatedly helped Dylan Thomas pay off his debts. He introduced young artists to more established artists and took them together to dinner. Stephen Spender called Peter "the last of a rare disinterested, pure and questing human species. No other patron was so individual, so non-institutional: even the word 'patron' seems wrong for him—perhaps a better word would be 'friend.'"[42]

He was, Spender felt, a knight in shining armor, a characterization that the Russian artist Pavel Tchelitchev had understood when he painted Peter as a knight.[43]

Peter went through periods when he found England

depressing, a "dying country"[44] as he called it, "a Victorian period piece,"[45] as the world, especially the world of modern art, moved beyond it. As Peter wrote to Cecil Beaton: "I am loathing London and can't wait to get out. The gloom. The cold. The bad plays."[46] He added: "There is some terrible psychological pain which gets me every time I get back to England. It goes back to the times when I used to race abroad to get away from my family I think."[47] He was considering founding in Paris a journal of fine arts, and also was sharing with Denny his idea of buying an orange farm in Arizona where the two of them would live. Paris won out and Peter leased the large apartment at 44 Rue du Bac.

It was in the summer of 1937, when Peter and Denny were staying in the fashionable Austrian ski resort town of Kitzbuhel, that they met up with Cyril Connolly who had been a student with Peter at Eton, and his wife Jean, an American expatriate just like Denny. Jean was beautiful, witty, caustic, a heavy drinker, sexy, promiscuous, a lover of clubs and late night parties, and she and Denny instantly bonded and became friends and confidants. ("Am suffering for *all* my sins at once with the most beastly (don't laugh) *WISDOM-TOOTH* while P. climbs Mts," Denny wrote to Jean on a postcard from the Hotel Glacier in Switzerland; "Love from Denham."[48] The Connollys often stayed at Peter's apartment when they were in Paris. They were there during the 1938 Christmas season, a time of typical chaos in the apartment that another guest remembered: "[It] had the air of a stage set, an extraordinary collection of people wandering in and out all day long, dubious friends of Denham's, English pansy or café society friends of the Connollys, the actor Jean Marais ...servants, detectives and police inspectors on account of a theft there at a party on Christmas Eve."[49] (Stephen Spender and his wife, Inez, when in Paris in 1938 and 1939, stayed at the apartment with Peter and Denny, always a little afraid of Denny after seeing several displays of his temper. On one occasion, as

Peter and Denny were arguing, Denny ran down the stairs out into the garden courtyard, fired a revolver into the air, came charging back into the apartment, and threw the empty revolver on a table.[50] Another time in a rage he drove a car straight toward the Seine, jumping clear just as it hit the water.)

As 1939 unfolded, the Connollys were having marital problems and Jean was spending more and more time in Paris, "Pansyhalla" as Cyril called it because his wife was seeing a lot of Peter and Denny and their friends. Peter wrote to Cyril: "Please get it out of your head that I want to see you and Jean separated. I do not and I should be very sorry if it happened and I only wish that a solution could be found and that you could be happy together, as I am fond of you both."[51]

At the end of August, Connolly—then, as the literary critic of the *New Statesman* and the literary editor of the *London Observer*, the most highly regarded and popular critic in Britain—returned to Paris to talk with Peter. When they sat down for lunch at a sidewalk café that hot summer afternoon, Peter realized that the topic on Cyril's mind was not Jean, but rather founding a new literary magazine in London. London's great literary reviews had gone out of existence—T.S. Eliot's *The Criterion, The London Mercury, New Verde*—and since 1938, with the gathering war clouds over Europe, many of England's artists and intellectuals had been seeking refuge in safer countries—W.H. Auden, Christopher Isherwood, Aldous Huxley, and Gerald Heard all had gone to the United States, Wyndham Lewis to Canada—and England was feeling, at least in Connolly's opinion, an intellectual and social drain.

Peter was cool to funding Connolly's proposal. He had no interest in leaving Paris to return to London, and his own plans for a journal on the fine arts were at last beginning to come together.

But Connolly's timing proved propitious. The next day, September 1, 1939, Germany invaded Poland and France. Two days later, Neville Chamberlain announced that Great Britain was at war with Germany. An air raid siren blared within minutes of his announcement, a warning that proved to be a false alarm though many fully expected "the sky to become black with bombers" with "the whole of London laid flat," as Stephen Spender remembered that ominous day.[52] An invasion of Paris seemed inevitable. Connolly returned to London.

Peter asked a Romanian acquaintance who lived in Paris to serve as the caretaker of his apartment while he was away for the duration of the trouble. He feared that his art collection might be confiscated by the Nazis and began to ship the masterpieces to London, including Picasso's *Girl Writing,* which was six feet high and four feet wide, had been in his collection for several years and was one of the most valuable. Fear in Paris of invasion was mounting so steadily that even before he could arrange for more paintings to be shipped, Peter left, leaving everything in his apartment, not even packing his luggage, and traveled from Paris to Calais aboard a troop train in a compartment filled with soldiers who "sat all the way in absolute silence, no one saying a word."[53] Denny had been traveling with Jean in Finland and reached London a few days after Peter. Peter was disgusted with both of them; as he told Cyril, if only they had moved faster when he told them to, they'd all be on their way to Mexico or Bali to sit out the war; Peter could have bought their way out for all of them. Now they all were stuck in London for the duration.

By the end of September, it was clear that no one would be returning to France in the near future, and Connolly again raised with Peter the idea of founding a literary magazine. Peter now viewed such a venture as a part of the war effort, an act of defiance in the face of the German threat, an undertaking that could be viewed as an effort to shore up the bulwarks of civilization, to defend culture. This time he agreed with Connolly's proposal and, on October 18, 1939, their venture began when Peter, as the financial backer and publisher, signed a contract to print the first four issues. In addition to funding the venture, Peter would be the art editor, responsible for securing essays and illustrations on modern art, and would help edit the issues. Cyril Connolly was the editor. Stephen Spender was selected by Peter to be assistant editor, primarily to try to stabilize the mercurial, and lazy, Connolly. And the associate editor on the masthead was: Denham Fouts. It wasn't long, a month, before Glenway Wescott in New York City received a letter from Denny in London "asking me to contribute and to solicit contributions to a magazine, *Horizon*."[54]

Peter had modest expectations for *Horizon*. He hoped that it would cover the expenses he was footing of printing the thousand copies of each issue and paying the staff salaries, fees to contributors, postage and advertising. As it happened, the journal was published with just the right formula at just the right time, and from the first issue, was a success. The pre-publication plans for a first printing of one thousand copies to be issued in January of 1940 increased to a run of 2,500. Every copy sold in a few days, as did another quick follow-up printing of 1,000 more. The second issue had a planned printing of 5,000 copies which was increased to 7,000 and which promptly sold out. *Horizon* built up to a circulation of 100,000 copies per issue, an unheard of figure for a literary magazine. The biggest problem, in fact, became securing enough paper with War rationing to print the magazine.

Peter loved his work because it afforded him another opportunity to discover and promote young artists by featuring their work in *Horizon*, with high quality reproductions and critical commentary. As Peter wrote to Cecil Beaton ("my dear Cee"), "What this country needs is *more and MORE* Art. Otherwise life is not worth the trouble. These are my War Aims and I am trying my best to attain them and shall continue to do so. Art must be put into everything—not just Writing, Painting, etc.; the whole World most swim with Art."[55]

Peter and Cyril worked well together and became close friends, with Cyril playfully calling Peter "Pierre" or "Peter Wattie," and Peter calling Cyril "Squirrel," "Papa," "Squiggles," or "Squig"; as another worker at *Horizon* noted, "they were almost in love with each other—very flirty."[56] But Peter's genius was in knowing how to stay in the background so that Cyril's genius would emerge and energize the magazine. "All I want you to do is to put in exactly what you like as you know I think your judgment is better than anyone else's, you silly thing; if I am asked an opinion I shall try to be sincere. My opinion about something is *not* a prohibition and I really resent it being taken as one."[57]

Cyril Connolly was *Horizon*. It reflected his moods, his opinions, his interests, his tastes. His work on the review made him something of a celebrity. "I think," he said, "the chill wind that blows from English publishers with their black suits and thin umbrellas, and their habit of beginning every sentence with 'We are afraid' has nipped off more promising buds than it has strengthened." It was Connolly's hope to encourage literary and artistic talent through *Horizon*. In setting his high standards as the benchmark for the magazine, he brought his audience up to those standards. "It was the right moment," Connolly said later, "to gather all the writers who could be preserved into the Ark."[58] And it was Connolly's genius, his intuition, to know who to solicit, and his charm that encouraged them to contribute to *Horizon*. And aboard the ark they came: T.S. Elliott, Aldous Huxley, Evelyn Waugh, Truman Capote, Philip Toynbee, Marshall McLuhan, Ralph Ellison, W.H. Auden, Edith Sitwell, Jean-Paul Sartre, C. Day Lewis, Stephen Randall Jarrell, E.E. Cummings, Wallace Stevens, John Berryman, Elizabeth Bowen, V.S. Pritchett, Kenneth Clark, Dylan Thomas, George Orwell. Peter soon saw that his own intuition had been correct, that Connolly is a "brilliant editor because he's like a brothel keeper, offering his writers to the public as though they were girls, and himself carrying on a flirtation with them."[59]

As the threat of invasion of Great Britain grew, Peter sent Denny to the United States to get him out of harm's way, away from the dangers of a war that now seemed inevitable, away from the easy access to drugs which had become increasingly important in his life. He had Denny bring with him for safe keeping Picasso's huge painting, *Girl Writing*.

On June 15, 1940, Denny and Jean Connolly set sail from Dublin for the United States.

CHAPTER FIVE

"A GENIUS FOR ENJOYING HIMSELF"

January 19, 1939.

"Well," Christopher Isherwood said as he boarded the French liner, *Champlain*, in Southampton, bound for New York, "we're off again."

"Goody," replied his travelling companion and friend since childhood, W.H. Auden.[1]

The two had heard the rumbles of war growing closer and been part of the artistic drain from England that so distressed Cyril Connolly and Peter Watson. The loss of these two men was especially devastating; Connolly considered Auden the country's "one poet of genius," and Isherwood as "the hope of English fiction."[2]

Auden adapted quickly to New York City, but Isherwood was baffled. "Oh God, what a city!" he wrote to his English publisher soon after arriving; "The nervous breakdown expressed in terms of architecture. The sky-scrapers are all Father-fixations. The police-cars are fitted with air-raid sirens, specially designed to promote paranoia. The elevated railway is the circular madness."[3] He hadn't a clue how he could earn a living there. And he was tormented by doubts about why he had left England. He considered himself a pacifist, but questioned why: were his beliefs sincere or was he really fleeing the dangers of serving his country?

A letter from Gerald Heard, a friend of Auden's who had met Isherwood in England, urged Christopher to come visit him in Los Angeles where he was studying Eastern mysticism, yoga and pacifism. Heard, who had been a science commentator for the BBC and the author of books on religion and human consciousness, had left England two years earlier with Aldous Huxley. Isherwood welcomed his invitation. "If you couldn't get hold of Bernard Shaw," Isherwood once said of Heard, "perhaps he was the next best thing ...the most fascinating person I've ever met."[4] With a desire to explore more deeply the core of his beliefs on war and peace, and with the hope that he could earn a living writing for the movies, Isherwood left on a Greyhound bus on a sightseeing trip across the country, arriving in Los Angeles later in May.

Isherwood found the dandy he remembered from England looking emaciated, sporting a long beard and a painter's smock over his dungarees and sneakers, and engaging in endless, though erudite and spell binding, monologues on pacifism and asceticism, spreading a gospel that "to become a true pacifist, you had to find peace within yourself; only then, he said, could you function pacifistically in the outside world."[5] Heard was a student of Vedanta, a Hindu philosophy, and followed a daunting regime of meditating six hours a day, interspersed with yoga and a diet, which consisted primarily of raisins, raw carrots, and tea. Isherwood was fascinated and receptive, and over the course of extended conversations, become intrigued by this Eastern religion. He had happened upon it at just the right time in his life. "To seek to realize my essential nature is to admit that I am dissatisfied with my nature as it is at present," Isherwood would write later when he had reached a point of being able to articulate what he was experiencing. "It is to admit that I am dissatisfied with the kind of life I am leading now."[6] Embracing this philosophy led to prolonged self analysis and reflection in an attempt to cease to be himself and to understand the very core of his being. When Heard felt Isherwood was ready, he introduced him to Swami Prabhavananda, a Hindu monk and the founder of the Vedanta Society of Southern California. At the same time, Isherwood found employment in Hollywood working on M-G-M movie scripts.

A year later, two more émigrés from England met up with Isherwood.

Denny and Jean had landed in New York City early in the summer of 1940, and on one of their whims took yoga classes together—and together, a few weeks later, made their way to Los Angeles. As Christopher Isherwood recalled it, on August 13 "a young American named Denny Fouts had arrived in Los Angeles."[7]

Isherwood invited Jean and Denny, along with a mutual friend, Tony Bower, an American film correspondent who had been introduced to Isherwood in 1937 by Jean and Cyril Connolly, to join him for lunch at the Beverly Brown Derby "with its atmosphere of overstuffed dullness and melancholy midday rum."[8] Christopher found Jean to be thinner than the last time he had seen her, "really beautiful with her big gentle cow eyes."[9] He looked at Denny as if examining an alien creature. As he wrote in his diary:

> If I try to remember how Denny struck me ...I think of the lean, hungry, tanned face, the eyes which seemed to be set on different levels, slightly overlapping, as in a late Picasso painting; the bitter little rosebud mouth; the strangely erect walk, almost paralytic with tension. He had rather sinister clothes—wash-leather jerkins, bell-bottomed sailor's trousers, boxer's sweaters. They were sinister because they were intended for laughing, harmless boys, not as a disguise for this tormented addict, this wolf-like inverted monk, this martyr to pleasure. His

good-looking profile was bitterly sharp, like a knife edge; his Floridian drawl seemed a sinister affection. Goodness he was sour! For a while, his sourness was stimulating: then you began to feel as if you were suffering from quinine poisoning.[10]

Denny described himself to Isherwood "as having been a spectacularly successful homosexual whore." Isherwood had heard that he had "had a number of affairs with rich men and that they had given him a lot of money. He made much of this, speaking of having been 'kept' by them, and watching your face as he used the word to see if you would wince."[11] Christopher later would realize that Denny "laid the whore act on rather thickly" and that, in many ways, he was very much like the Sally Bowles character in the novel he had written the year before, *Goodbye to Berlin*: "they both tended to play-act their lives."[12] Both Jean and Denny had hangovers when Christopher met them, "which they nursed with the greatest satisfaction; while steadily tanking up for the next blind."[13]

Isherwood would turn thirty-five later that month. Already an acclaimed author, his fiction was regarded as avant garde, groundbreaking, at the forefront of a new school of literature— the documentary novel. At the beginning of *Goodbye to Berlin*, (much later popularized as the musical and film *Cabaret*), Isherwood wrote his famous line: "I am a camera with its shutter open, quite passive, recording, not thinking." Indeed, the basis of all his writing was autobiography, and he placed himself—often as a character named "Christopher," or even "Christopher Isherwood"—in much of his fiction. His diaries and memoirs contain the contemporaneous material that would become his novels, and the novella he would write about Denny is like a home movie of their lunch that day in August, and a recording of their next five years together. It was in 1949 that Isherwood first contemplated writing a short story about Denny, but not until March of 1956 that his ideas about Denny had begun to crystallize so that he could write to a friend: "As regards the novel, I have started it—half a page! Virgil is definitely to be Denny Fouts."[14] He would work on this book for four more years.

"Paul," the fourth and final section of what would become this novel, *Down There on a Visit*, opens in the autumn of 1940 with the narrator, named Christopher, in a restaurant in Los Angeles having lunch with Ronny, a character based on Tony Bower, Ruthie, who was Jean Connolly, and Paul, who was now Denny, and so is the camera-like account of the author's first encounter with Denham Fouts. In *Down There on a Visit*, the author provides a snapshot of Denny as Paul, almost a word-for-word repetition of his first entry about Denny in his diaries:

> the lean, hungry-looking tanned face, the eyes which seemed to be set on different levels, as in a Picasso painting; the bitter, well-formed mouth. His handsome profile was bitterly sharp, like a knife edge. And goodness, underneath the looks and the charm and the drawl, how sour he was! The sourness of Paul's could sometimes be wonderfully stimulating and bracing, especially as an antidote to sweetness and light. But I learned by experience to take it in cautious doses. Too much of it at one time could make you feel as if you were suffering from quinine poisoning.[15]

Isherwood's video-prose captures Paul's/Denny's "strangely erect walk; he seemed almost paralytic with tension. He was always slim, but then he looked boyishly skinny; and he was dressed like a boy in his teens, with an exaggerated air of innocence which he seemed to be daring us to challenge." In the story, we see Paul/Denny "in his drab black suit, narrow-chested and without shoulder padding, clean white shirt and plain black tie [that] made him look as if he had just arrived in town from a strictly religious boarding school. His dressing so young didn't strike me as ridiculous, because it went with his appearance. Yet, since I knew he was in his late twenties, this youthfulness itself had a slightly sinister effect, like something uncannily preserved."[16]

The author's camcorder prose caught the sound of Denny's voice as having a "peculiar drawling tone, which is probably the result of mixing a Southern accent with the kind of pseudo-Oxford English spoken by cultured Europeans—the people he has been running around with during the past few years."[17]

These descriptions of Paul in the novel faithfully mirror Isherwood's first impressions of Denny recorded in his diary. His portrayal of Paul's character is just as faithful a depiction of Denny's character.

At the chapter's opening lunch, Paul is playing it cool, trying to act unimpressed by the fact that he is dining with a well known writer who is making good money in Hollywood, and, at the same time, trying to catch Christopher's attention. Paul's legend has preceded him, and the narrator is very much aware that this boyishly handsome man across the table is "the most expensive male prostitute in the world"; the narrator asks himself, "Do I care? Part of me already disapproves of Paul; part of me is bored by the tedious naughtiness of his legend. But, so far, I haven't reached my verdict. I'm waiting to see if he'll do anything to interest me; and I almost believe he knows this. I feel, at any rate, that he's capable of knowing it. That's what intrigues me about him."[18]

This exploration of character is at the heart of Isherwood's chapter: a study of Paul, and so, of Denny, penetrating deep into the psyche of this unusual individual. As he worked on his book, the author's aim was "to keep to the fore the whole relationship between Paul & me. I see it as a sort of dialogue, a love-affair on the metaphysical plane. Something that goes deeper than surface-personality."[19] The

54

story is a study of subtle human interaction, of those who, thinking they know someone, make certain assumptions about him, and of their willingness, or unwillingness, to alter those assumptions as circumstances shift. While the narrator watches Paul change, or seem to change, his understanding of Paul changes, develops, solidifies, then changes once again, and then again, as this quiet narrative unfolds.

At the lunch, Christopher senses that Paul is trying to impress him and realizing this, acts as if he is bored by Paul. The conversation turns to Christopher's study of yoga with Augustus Parr, a well known guru—a character Isherwood closely modeled after Gerald Heard. Paul mentions that he has read a book of Parr's. This arouses Christopher's curiosity, the two begin talking about the book, and Christopher is floored by Paul's perceptive remarks about it.

This was just as it happened. Isherwood had at first found Denny tiresome, but became intrigued when he showed a sincere interest in Vedanta and the Swami. "Long conversations with him had gradually convinced me that his interest was absolutely serious. It seemed to be related to some terrifying insights he had had while taking drugs."[20]

In the novel, Christopher asks Paul how long he's been interested in this subject. "I never said I was *interested.* As a matter of fact, I think all that stuff's a lot of crap. I *know* it is." Their prickly exchange continues on, and Christopher, fed up, hopes never to see Paul again.

Two weeks later, Paul calls him at the Hollywood studio where he works, telling him that Ruthie misses him, and adding "I want to see you, too." Christopher is ready to brush him off when Paul utters the magic words: "You're the only one who can help me, Christopher."[21] This caught Christopher's attention (just as Glenway Wescott knew it would when, years before in New York City, he had advised Denny how to work his way into someone's life). Paul insisted that he couldn't discuss the matter on the phone, that

Christopher would have to come to the bungalow that he, Ruthie, and Ronny were renting.

When he arrived, Ruthie and Paul were sunbathing, nude, on mattresses around the edge of an empty pool, and three young men, Marines, were there with them, in underwear and swim trunks, drinking beer. Paul told Christopher to take off his clothes: "If you don't, Ruth'll think you're ashamed of your small pecker."[22] Fed up with Paul's teasing and testing banter, Christopher announces he is leaving. At this point, Paul walks with him into the house and gets right to the point, asking Christopher if he believed any of what they were talking about the other week at lunch. The two start debating eastern philosophy, Christopher explaining it, Paul challenging it, at times seeming to heckle Christopher, at other times seeming sincerely interested. ("What makes you think it's [life] *for* anything?" Paul questions: "Why can't it just be a filthy mess of meaningless shit?")[23] In the course of the conversation, Christopher reveals that he's begun mediating, which fascinates Paul and leads to further questioning. ("So you just sit there? I know I'd start thinking about all the people I'd had in my entire life. I'd end by jacking myself off.")[24] Christopher patiently described how "you sit there, and, all of a sudden, you know you're face to face with something. You can't see it, but it's right there." Paul is curious, but skeptical. "Well, personally, I've always stuck to what I can see and touch and smell and grope and screw. That's all you can really trust. The rest's just playing around with words until you talk yourself into something. I don't say these mystics of yours are deliberate fakes. But they can't prove to me that they're not kidding themselves."[25]

Here continues the debate—both explicit and implicit—that runs through this story, a debate between the spiritual side of life, represented by the new world Christopher is discovering, and the earthy side of the world, represented by Paul's past, a past of groping and screwing. Why, Christopher questions, had Paul asked him to come that afternoon: "What was it you wanted to talk to me about?" "Nothing," Paul answers.[26]

But several nights later, long after he is asleep, Christopher's telephone rings. It is Paul, sounding distraught, telling him he will be there in fifteen minutes. He arrives, disheveled, dirty, with one eye blackened. He has been in a fight with one of the Marines Christopher had seen around the pool the afternoon he visited; Paul says he has fallen out with Ruthie and Ronny and realizes "they simply hate my guts. So I told them I was getting out. And I got out."[27] Paul has with him a bottle of sleeping pills he has stolen from Ronny, and is making references to killing himself. "Until yesterday evening," Paul explains, "there was always something left to stop me from being certain—some tiny little things, like feeling curious about a movie we were going to see, or about what I'd eat for dinner, or just what was going to happen next. Well, yesterday I suddenly found I'd come to the end of all that."[28] Pretty thin reeds to keep oneself alive, and Christopher, not at all sure that Paul's declaration is anything more than late night theatrics, asks why he doesn't just take the pills, asking him if he is too scared to do it. "Hell, no! Not that. Scared of what's going to happen afterwards."[29] He is concerned that what is after death might be worse than the present. Christopher tests him: "Then don't risk it. Stay alive." Paul reveals the depth of his emptiness:

> "I used to be good for something—for sex. I was *really* good for that. All kinds of people used to get hot pants for me, and that excited me—even when I found them totally unattractive, which I usually did. I got a terrific kick out of giving them pleasure, and was proud that I nearly always could. But then, by degrees, the whole thing got more and more frantic. I began to feel I'd got to go on and on and on having sex, even

when I was exhausted. And then I realized I loathed sex. I was trying to screw it right out of my system."[30]

Paul admits that he has been impotent for several months. "I mean absolutely impotent. I can't even get it hard."[31] He had tried to cover up his condition, but Ruthie and Ronny had found out. Christopher taunts him, assuming that this midnight confession is simply another of Paul's cries for attention. "We're all supposed to fall down on our asses with amazement because you're such a devilishly wicked Dorian Gray. Actually, you're a rather vulgar little not-so-young boy from the most unpleasant state in the Union, whose chief claim to sophistication is having been thrown out of a few European hotels."[32] At that outburst, Paul stalks from the apartment, and Christopher, concerned that he may have misjudged him and gone too far, runs after him and leads him back inside. The two have breakfast, and Christopher calls his guru, Augustus Parr, to make an immediate appointment for him to meet with Paul.

The yogi spends the day with Paul. In their meditations, Paul goes through a violent sort of catharsis, rolling on the floor, crying in spasms, and finally relaxing, asking Augustus Parr, "Why did you do that to me?"[33] Augustus reports to Christopher that "there's a very curious expression in the eyes—you see it sometimes in photographs of wild animals at bay. But one also saw something else—which no animal has or can have—despair. Not helpless, negative despair. Dynamic despair. The kind that makes dangerous criminals, and, very occasionally, saints."[34] How close those two extremes are Isherwood explores in this story, how they can shift and flicker back and forth. Augustus Parr tells Christopher that he feels progress has been made during his day spent with Paul, but that only Christopher can help him.

The next morning Christopher is awakened by a call from Ronny to go bail Paul out of jail; he had wrecked his car that night and been arrested for drunk driving. Christopher realizes that, for better or worse, he is stuck with Paul, that Paul is his problem. He learns that Paul has no money, that he has expected to "live off Ruthie, I guess. Till someone else showed up."[35] That day, as he meditates, Christopher wonders "Does anything happen by accident? Augustus said No. Paul and I had met because we needed each other. Yes, now I suddenly saw that; I needed Paul every bit as much as he needed me. Our strength and our weakness were complimentary. It would be much easier for us to go forward together than separately. Only it was up to me to take the first step."[36] Christopher, through his meditation, feels a brotherly love for Paul. He invites him to stay at his apartment, and, inspired, gives him half of all the money he has in his bank account, with no strings attached.

And so began the characters' monastic, celibate life together, which mirrors Christopher's and Denny's months together, beginning with an hour of meditation at six a.m., followed by breakfast, then lessons when they read aloud to each other from a book recommended by their yogi, more meditation at noon, a light lunch, a walk or drive ("while we were in the car, the one who wasn't driving would read aloud to the other. This was supposed to distract our minds and eyes from attractive pedestrians; actually, it had the opposite effect; our glances became furtively compulsive and we had several near collisions"[37]), a vegetarian supper. "This was certainly one of the happiest periods of my life. The longer I lived with Paul, the more I became aware of a kind of geisha quality in him; he really understood how to give pleasure, to make daily life more decorative and to create enjoyment of small occasions."[38] This was, in fact, precisely Denny's gift.

While Paul is at the dentist one morning, Christopher takes a call for him from the Railway Express office that "they had a picture to deliver." Paul knows what it is: "'Oh, sure— that's my Picasso,' he said casually. 'They've certainly taken their time getting it here, I must say. It was stored in New York. I sent for it soon after I moved in with you. It'll brighten the place up a bit.'" When it arrives it is "enormous—at least for our apartment—over six feet long and about four feet wide; a tall narrow painting of a giant girl seated at a high-legged table. The girl had a violet face, two noses, hands like the wings of birds and a crown of pale poisonous-looking flowers."

"Good God!" I exclaimed. "It really *is* a Picasso!"

"Well, *of course*, it is, honey chile! Did you think your old Aunt would tote a reproduction around? This is my last and only souvenir of Europe.'" In the novel, the Condesa has given it to Paul just before he left for the United States. "'It used to hang in her bedroom and I always liked to wake up with it in the morning ...'"[39]

Christopher and Paul go together on a ten day retreat with Augustus Parr and twelve more of his followers to a campsite near Palm Springs. With the group were two beautiful teenage girls, one of whom, Dee-Ann, begins flirting with Paul, wrestling with him, telling him: "Do you know what Alanna said about you once? She said you were beautiful,"[40] riding horses with him, swimming with him. On the last day of the retreat, Alanna goes to her parents and tells them she has "seen Paul with Dee-Ann, through the window of [Christopher's] cabin, in an act of sex."[41] Paul then is seen speeding away from the site in Christopher's car. When he returns, Paul is confronted, and doesn't deny the allegations. Paul accuses Christopher of making his mind up about what has happened based on what others have told him, even before he has spoken with him. On the drive back to Los Angeles, Paul tells Christopher that he hasn't done anything. "But, Paul, wait a minute—why did you tell them you'd done it?" Christopher asks. "I did not tell them. I just didn't deny it. And why the hell should I? They all believed I did it from the word go. They were just hearing what they'd been expecting to hear all along."[42] Dee-Ann's sister later confesses that Dee-Ann has fabricated the entire story.

Paul, who has filed as a conscientious objector, receives an order from his draft board directing him to report to forestry camp. At the camp, Paul is a favorite of the others who are fascinated by his tales of Europe and by his dog, Gigi, the only dog in the camp, "huge and shaggy and sloppy-tongued,"[43] but the Quaker directors of the camp are quite concerned about Paul's habit of playfully addressing the others as "Darling ... and ... Lover Boy"; they are relieved to discover he has a heart murmur, which they use as reason to have him, after two years at the camp, reclassified as 4-F and discharged.

On their ride home from the camp, Paul questions Christopher about whether he is still dedicated to the principles of yoga and learns that Christopher is now taking a more relaxed approach, meditating only on occasion, not following a strictly vegetarian diet, and having sex whenever he feels like it. Paul chastises Christopher for reverting to just what he was before he began to alter his life, and tells him, "I know what I *really* want now. I discovered that up at camp. I don't want any more of this auto hypnotism and professional goodness. I'm sick of trying to imagine I feel things. I just want to *know*."[44] He tells Christopher he has decided to become a psychoanalyst, that he has taken correspondence courses while at camp and gotten his high school diploma, that he'll be starting a pre-med program in New York City in the fall, and that he will be leaving in a few days. Christopher is astounded. "Paul," I said, and I meant it, "you're the most amazing person I know."[45]

Augustus Parr also is astonished, delighted at the news. "That will of his!" Augustus exclaimed. "My word! It would move mountains undoubtedly."[46] Christopher isn't so sure Paul will be able to follow through and complete the necessary courses. "For I had just realized one fact about his motivations: he could only do things—even altogether constructive things, like getting a medical degree—*against* someone else. There always had to be an enemy, whose role it was to lack faith in Paul and be proved wrong. And Paul's latest enemy wasn't the Quakers or Augustus, or the people he had known in Europe, or Ruthie or Ronny; it was me."[47]

It isn't until the summer of 1946 that Christopher receives a letter from Paul, telling him that he has sold the Picasso, that he is leaving New York and going to Europe "perhaps for a long while," and that he has given up medical school "because I have realized that I'll never be a good psychologist until I've understood certain things for myself. I don't mean just by getting myself analyzed; I mean by living through them again."[48] Christopher later hears from friends in Europe that Paul is being seen in all his regular haunts "doing all the usual things with the usual people."[49] Christopher wonders if Paul had gained anything from their sojourn together.

This quiet story is an exploration of how reality can emerge only through the diminution of self. Paul is there to test, to challenge, to poke at the new reality Christopher thinks he is discovering. Once, in a lecture, Isherwood said that "Paul is a touchstone of sincerity, without meaning to be ... without being any better himself, he has the most awful faculty of exposing that tiny little bit of untruth that there is in almost all of us."[50] There are no absolutes in the story, no moral judgments. In an interview in 1961, Isherwood called the book "a loosely constructed fictional autobiography, something in the manner of *Goodbye to Berlin*,"[51] and in an interview ten years later, he continued this analogy, comparing Paul/Denny to Sally Bowles.[52]

The plot of "Paul" follows precisely Christopher's own experiences with Denny from their first lunch at the Beverly Brown Derby restaurant in Los Angeles with Jean Connolly and Tony Bower. Isherwood found that Denny wished to make a clean break with the life he had been leading in Europe before the War, and a few weeks after their first meeting recorded his thoughts in his diary:

> Lunch with Denny, who is anxious to start a new life as soon as the Swami gets back. He means to take a big plunge—get a shack in the hills, a menial job (as somebody's servant) and immediately renounce everything: sex, drink, and the Gang. He's very nervous and much worried about his motives—is he wishing to do this for the right reasons? But surely, at the start, the reasons don't matter? If you are doing this for the wrong reasons, I told him, you'll very soon find out. Meanwhile, Denny still goes to parties and gets drunk and talks nothing but religion, to the great amusement of Tony Bower and Jean Connolly, who call him "the drunken yogi."[53]

By later in October of 1940, Christopher thought Denny ready for a visit to the Vedanta temple and together they sat in the shrine. "I couldn't concentrate," Christopher remembers, "I was thinking all the time of Denny—hoping he wouldn't be put off by the photographs on the shrine, and the flowers, and the ivory and brass figures of Krishna, Buddha and Shiva. It *does* look rather like the mantelpiece in an old-fashioned boudoir. Actually, Denny liked it all very much, but was dismayed because he had thought what a wonderful place it would be to have sex in."[54]

Isherwood acknowledged in his diaries that he "had become possessive of Denny, regarding him as my personal convert, the soul I had saved."[55] Certainly his conversion of such an infamous character, such a notorious reprobate, would have impressed his guru and added immeasurably to his stature in the eyes of Swami Prabhavananda. But Denny's meeting with Isherwood's guru was a disaster: "he must have been aggressive and theatrical and strident, painting himself as the lowest of sinners and daring Prabhavananda to reject him." The guru told him that what he really needed was not spiritual guidance but to go out and get a job, to work. Isherwood records that "Denny was terribly disappointed and hurt. As soon as we got back to his room, he threw himself down on the bed and burst into tears, sobbing that he was rotten, everybody despised him, and he'd better kill himself with heroin as soon as possible ..."[56] Christopher tried to calm him. "I protested, of course—as anybody would. In fact, I said far more than I meant. I told him that *I* didn't despise him, that I admired him and liked him and wanted to be his friend. This episode had very far-reaching consequences ...It ...involved me with Denny—so that, in a little while, I really did become very fond of him."[57]

To carry out Swami's recommendation, Gerald Heard arranged for Denny to work at an organic farm in Pennsylvania so that Denny could learn the principles of farming and then help put them into practice in the monastic community that Gerald was planning. While he was at the farm, Denny sent daily letters to Gerald and Christopher. "Denny was trying to live entirely without sex, and his lurid accounts of his temptations and struggles made Gerald exclaim repeatedly, 'My word, what a tough!' Denny was certainly the white-haired boy of our little circle. We all went around discussing him, raving about him and dwelling with frissons of excitement on the awful life of sin he had lived before his 'change.' We were pretty ridiculous, no doubt—like church spinsters cooing over a converted burglar."[58]

By the spring of 1941, Denny, who despised the farmer and everything about life on the farm, returned to California, and Isherwood invited him to stay at his apartment until he was drafted. Isherwood reasoned that it would be good to live with Denny "because he's the only person who can view my life as a whole, and therefore the only one who can give me any valuable advice. He isn't shocked by the squalid bits of it, and he isn't repelled or mystified by Vedanta." There of course was a downside to living with Denny: "Denny's company is very disturbing to me, a lot of the time. Because his life is free, bohemian, agreeable and full of affairs."[59] With Isherwood's declaration of friendship with no sexual strings attached—the sort of friendship Denny had never before known—Denny expressed his determination "to start meditating and living 'intentionally.'"[60]

The two had decided to undertake together what they called an experiment in "intentional living." Their days together fell into a pleasing routine. When the morning alarm rang, Christopher awakening in his bedroom and Denny in the living room each began an hour of meditation. Denny then washed, dressed, and prepared breakfast ("he was," Isherwood commented, "an inventive cook and he had the knack of homemaking"[61]), while Christopher washed and dressed. At that time, the silence was broken when they said "good morning." After doing the dishes and whatever housekeeping was necessary, they read to each other from a religious text, books like William James' *Varieties of Religious Experience*, books that they often criticized and mocked. "*Mary*, how pretentious can you get?" and "How she *dare*!", were among Denny's favorite put-downs of the authors.[62] About God, Denny once said, "I have no need for that hypothesis."[63] Like Paul in *Down There on a Visit*, he always was detecting inconsistencies and dishonesties in what people said, and was quick to pin someone as a phony. Christopher at times "egged Denny on in order to be able to enjoy the contrast of someone even sourer than myself."[64]

The second hour of meditation commenced at noon, followed by lunch. As in "Paul," "If we went out in the car during the afternoon, we took our book with us and the nondriver read it to the driver. This was supposed to keep us from watching for sexy pedestrians. It didn't, but it did divide the driver's attention by three—book, pedestrian, road—

instead of by two, and was therefore cause of several near accidents."[65] The third hour of meditation was from six to seven o'clock, followed by supper and to bed by nine-thirty. "We had agreed that we would give up sex, including masturbation. This was made easier by the fact that we didn't find each other in the least sexually attractive. However, while keeping to the agreement, we talked about sex constantly, boasting of our past conquests and adventures."[66]

Isherwood would look back on these days with Denny as among the most joyful in his life. "On the whole, those weeks of May and June were unexpectedly happy ... The day lived itself, our timetable removed all anxieties about what we should be doing next. We were continually occupied, and everything we did seemed enjoyable and significant. The apartment was curiously delightful to be in, because of the atmosphere we were creating. I don't remember our having one real quarrel."[67]

Isherwood came to see that there was no one more fun to be with than Denham Fouts. In everything he did, Denny could reveal to others the wonder of being alive, he could find the extraordinary in the most ordinary parts of the day. Like Paul in Christopher's novella, Denny could make "the marketing seem fascinatingly important; he chose fruits and vegetables as carefully as if they were neckties or socks."[68] Isherwood would later remember these months when "we really relied on each other"[69] as "some of the happiest of my whole life.[70] Everything we did seemed interesting and amusing. The apartment acquired a kind of nursery atmosphere of innocence."[71]

Their friends had doubts about what they were doing, convinced that after a number of weeks they would come to their senses and realize all the religious mumbo jumbo they were spouting was so much nonsense. They especially hoped "that Denny will have a relapse and return to his old ways. Denny causes more resentment than any of us because he is a traitor to the gang, and because everybody had him so neatly taped as a drunken, doping sex maniac. Denny's desertion is very disturbing."[72] Isherwood felt that "Denny contributed more to the success of our experiment than I did, both materially and morally ... As I now see, this was because he had much more to lose than I had if we failed. This was the last bridge he hadn't burned ..."[73]

Through Aldous Huxley, they found a teacher of hatha-yoga exercises, which they practiced "for purely athletic reasons; ...the exercise did make us feel wonderfully healthy."[74] Christopher's Swami disapproved of these lessons.

"'What is the matter with you, Mr. Isherwood?' he asked me reproachfully, 'surely you do not want Eternal Youth?'

I was silent and hung my head—because, of course, I did."[75]

Like any eager beginner learning a new skill, Denny in those spring days of 1941 kept careful notes of his first meeting with their yoga instructor, who, as Isherwood described, "though perhaps a lot older than she looked, was the embodiment of suppleness and serpentine charm."[76] Their lessons were each Thursday afternoon at 4:30 p.m., and Denny in his notebook recorded just what they were to practice on their own:

stretches—prone 3 ea
alternate breathing sitting cross-legged, separate nostrils.
At end hold breath long as pos. let out slowly 12 rounds
Balance on Coccyx—shakes—(tuch up) 6 rounds
Spine-rock (ironing) (many as we like)
Abdominal on elbows with knee up—*20 times swallow air* before
Same on hands and knees (cat hump)

Their instructor, they found, was "a perfect lady" who "never lost her social poise. Having explained that the air which is passed through the body in the air-swallowing exercise should come out 'quite odorless' she merely smiled in playful reproach when we discharged vile-smelling farts."[77]

Another page of Denny's handwritten notes sketched out a regime of alternate breathing exercises, from the "Hollow tank (3)," the "Jackknife—6 at least to 12 as many as we can," to a shoulder stand and "abdominals—swallow air + water—prone on elbows, knees up (20) + cat hump—(20)." For the next lesson on Tuesday at four o'clock they were to read the book "*Heaven Lie Within Us*—Bernard." Another session featured the "cork-screw rock," the "inch worm from above into snake + back," and the "snake posture," all of which was to be practiced "1/2 hr morning and 1/2 hr evening." Denny's notes for another routine began with: "1. Run on beach—swim if warm enough," to "a chair + stool push-up" to "Belly punch," "the tuch" and "beauty roll."

The lessons became more advanced. As Christopher noted: "Our teacher began to urge us to learn the yoga technique of washing out the intestines by muscular action alone; you squat in a bowl full of water, suck the water in through the anus, swirl it around inside you, expel it again, thus cleansing yourself of poisons. Until this technique had been mastered you should use an enema everyday. And meanwhile, the sphincter muscle of the anus must be made more flexible, through dilation ... A set of rectal dilators now appeared. The largest was a wicked-looking dildo, quite beyond my capacity but dangerously tempting to my curiosity. I told Denny that, at least as far as I was concerned, our lessons would have to stop—lest sex should sneak in through the back door."[78] That ended their formal sessions, but they continued some of the exercises they had learned.

It was not surprising that, living with an author, Denny was beguiled by the writer's life and the potential monetary rewards of telling stories; surely he had lived more than a lifetime's worth of fiction. It was during these idyllic days with Christopher, between meditating and exercising, that he tried his hand at writing a novel.

"Chap. I" he wrote in his confident, neat script on a page of lined school notebook paper, and then began:

> Two men [Denny crossed out those first two words and gave the two men names, inserting Eduardo and Sefton]—watched the New York plane take form in the early morning California haze and settle in front of the Glendale Airport. They both had hangovers and had eaten no breakfast but were drinking splits of sour domestic champagne on the visitors Terrace to celebrate Prim's arrival.[79]

The two men had anticipated this moment and had dressed the part for Prim's benefit since she jokingly had accused them of having "gone Hollywood."

Denny's amateur, first draft efforts become apparent in the next few overwritten sentences; he is dealing with an interesting insight but is having trouble weaving it into the narrative. In describing how the men dressed for Prim, he wrote:

> This was more than affectation, however, and in fact formed a fundamental aspect of their whole attitude toward America. For, although they were citizens, they had spent most of their lives abroad, and when the war reminded them forcibly of their birthright, their resentment at having to take advantage of it knew no bounds. They openly pretended to a tolerant but incorruptible hatred of everything American to cover up the guilt of their compromise with a profound aversion to their roots. California was considered to contain a more concentrated essence of the "soul destroying" qualities of

69

America then [sic] anywhere else. Eduardo and Sefton's clothes were to indicate that, although immersed, they were immune and could still laugh with the most contemptuous.

At the bottom right corner of this first page, and each page thereafter of the manuscript, Denny carefully recorded his word count.

Prim gets off the plane in an outfit that more than matched the mens': high-heeled sandals made of clear plastic, red pajamas, and large sunglasses. Again, Denny analyzes the scene: "This combination suggested to all three the ultimate esoteric comment on Hollywood, and so exquisitely complimented the sartorial efforts of the two men that for a while they floated giddily on a wave of mirth which carried them high above their individual considerations, isolating them from the rest of the world in an impenetrable cell of sly, superior intimacy."

Rather than telling a story, rather than letting his characters' personalities emerge through their actions and words and having a narrative unfold through the characters, Denny is filling in the missing pieces for the reader, and in doing so, is bogging down the story. "Prim rather fancied herself in her 'get-up,' however, and no flattery was ever too gross to be absorbed by a physical vanity which was the only portion of her ego that Eduardo and Sefton provided no nourishment for whatsoever. It was the only deficiency in their relationship and what disharmony existed between them was chiefly caused by Prim's extra-relational satisfaction of this need and the two men's resentment and ridicule of it."

The three climb into Eduardo's new Cadillac roadster. It becomes clear through their conversation that Eduardo and Prim have been lovers, sharing "spells of almost religious intimacy—that is, when they were not actually fighting," though we learn a little later that Prim is married to a RAF officer who has been missing in action in Libya, though none of the three friends "could care less if he was dead or alive." As they drive along Hollywood Boulevard, Eduardo concedes that the roadster isn't paid for but that he was given the tires by a man who has asked Eduardo to cash some checks in the East, which Eduardo in turn has sent to Prim to put through her bank account; for his efforts in laundering this money, the man gave him a choice of tires and Eduardo buys the roadster to go with the new tires. Eduardo knows little about the man, other than "everyone in Hollywood knows him" and that the man knew Eduardo's mother. Eduardo, the reader learns, is her only child, the son of her first husband who died on the Titanic. "(Lusitania?)" Denny writes in a parenthetical, a decision he would have to make later.

Eduardo's mother "knew everyone in Europe, and that included Kings, Dictators and Prime Ministers. Her very intimate and indiscriminate relationships in this powered category was inexplicable to most people except in highly romantic terms and she was universally looked upon as a Dangerous Woman." As the novel opens, she is living in Portugal and will not return to the United States until her protégé, a young Greek poet, receives a visa; although many of her friends assume the two are having an affair, the young poet is, as Denny describes him, "thoroughly homosexual." Although she has never been close to her son, she is relying now on Eduardo to help her secure a visa for Niko, the poet.

Eduardo pulls the roadster into a parking lot and the three get out of the car just as a chauffeur in the parking lot opened the door of a gray Rolls Royce for a "small dark bald-headed jew dressed entirely in white"; Prim recognizes him and calls out "Pepe!" Pepe knows Eduardo also and asks Eduardo to join him in the Rolls so that they can talk as he is driven downtown. Reluctantly, Eduardo gets in Pepe's car.

As Chapter 2 opens, Prim and Sefton follow their porter past a swimming pool to a bungalow, where apparently the three of them will be staying. They pour themselves drinks, and as Sefton watches Prim, "a great rush, of tenderness for her filled his heart, overwhelming him." Denny continues: "'Prim, darling, I do adore you," he said feelingly as he snuggled down next to her. "This horrid place and all the boring [here Denny crossed out the word "boring" and inserted "horrid"] people—I can't tell you, it's too ghastly." As Prim strokes Sefton's hair, Sefton admits he is concerned about Eduardo, that he is acting differently.

Here the manuscript text gets out-of-order, and on a blank page Denny has written "notebooks like Chris," perhaps a recognition of the value to Isherwood of his diary of daily jottings, observations, snatches of dialogue, character sketches that could be worked into a novel or feed a writer's imagination.

The pages pick up with Sefton in a bar having dinner with a character named Boney, who, Sefton learns, is in California to arrest Pepe. Pepe, Boney explains to Sefton, is a spy involved in a Nazi sabotage plot: to dump a load of high explosives at Consolidated Aircraft sometime Tuesday night; Pepe would be there himself to master mind the plot, and would be arrested. At the same time, as Sefton is meeting with Boney, Eduardo and Prim are having lunch on the terrace with an unnamed king.

And there, after the sixty-eighth handwritten notebook page, ends the first and only draft of Denny's novel.

Certainly Denny has introduced some characters and some plot lines with the potential to build a novel. The relationships between Eduardo, Sefton, and Prim are ambiguous, which lends a tension to the text. We know that Prim is married to a missing-in-action RAF officer and has also some romantic feelings for Eduardo. In the car, Eduardo puts his arm around Prim, "cuddling her in an extravagant display of affection which characterized their behavior toward each other in between their spells of almost religious intimacy." Sefton, too, feels close to Prim: "Oh, Prim, darling, I do adore you," Sefton had said to Prim, "feelingly as he snuggled down next to her." It's not yet clear what feelings Eduardo and Sefton may have for each other; in the car, "Sefton ruffles Eduardo's hair and laughs happily like a child," and, learning for the first time what Eduardo has done to get the new tires, Sefton "gave Eduardo's head a little push." Prim tells Sefton he should go away on a little vacation, and Sefton responds that "I don't want to go anywhere unless Eddie comes with me." Then there is the mysterious, secret agent man, Pepe, who has used Eduardo to launder money and may be involved in a Nazi sabotage plot, and Eduardo's mother, who sounds very much like a female version of Denham Fouts, she who "knew everyone in Europe, and that included Kings, Dictators and Prime Ministers," someone who was "universally looked upon as a Dangerous Woman."

In these opening pages, Denny has set in motion a cast of characters able to carry several lines of intrigue, all of which could have been woven together into a novel: the relationship between the three friends; what Eduardo was doing for Pepe and why; whether Pepe was a Nazi sympathizer and would be exposed; whether Eduardo's mother would get the visa for her protégé; how these different plot lines would intersect and resolve themselves.

All the seeds were there to germinate into a novel, but as Robert Louis Stevenson knew, this was just about as far as any amateur could get: "There must be something for hope to feed upon," the great novelist wrote; "The beginner must have a slant of wind, a lucky vein must be running, he must be in one of those hours when the words come and the phrases balance of themselves—even to begin. And having begun, what a dread looking forward is that until the book shall be accomplished!" As Stevenson added: "Anybody can write a short story—a bad one, I mean—who has industry and paper and time enough; but not everyone may hope to write even a bad novel. It is the length that kills ... Human nature has certain rights; instinct—the instinct of self-preservation—forbids that any man (cheered and supported by the consciousness of no previous victory) should endure the miseries of unsuccessful literary toil beyond a period to be measured in weeks. There must be something for hope to feed upon."[80] Like countless before him, Denny concluded after drafting a chapter or two that the writer's life was not all it seemed, and certainly not as easy as it seemed, and, for him, not worth the effort.

These days of bliss, of living intentionally, ended on August 21, 1941, when Denny, who, like Paul, had filed as a conscientious objector, was called to report to a forestry camp in the mountains of San Dimas, about twenty miles outside of Los Angeles. "We spent a melancholy two weeks buying his ugly trousseau," Christopher wrote in his diary, "the stiff blue denim work clothes and the clumsy boots ... I drove him as far as Glendora, where the camp director's wife would come down to fetch him. As we approached the scene of parting, Denny began to talk nostalgically about Paris, and his former loves and triumphs."[81]

Like Paul in Isherwood's novel, Denny became a favorite of the others at the forestry camp. From the start, he enjoyed his months there, happy to find, as Isherwood noted, that "he could get along in a group and be accepted and popular. He spent money wildly, on all kinds of luxury equipment—waterproof wristwatches, super-sleeping-bags, fur-lined jackets—for himself and as presents for his friends."[82] Denny adopted a stray dog wandering around the camp, "huge and shaggy and sloppy-tongued," just like Gigi in the novel. Trotsky became his life companion. Denny was the cook for the camp and in his free time was studying correspondence courses through UCLA to get his high school diploma, with the plan of then following a program of higher education to become a psychiatrist.

The directors of the camp weren't quite certain what to make of such a worldly free spirit who had no regard for routines or authority. They reported to Isherwood that Denham Fouts was a "subversive influence"[83] and accused him of bringing liquor and marijuana into the camp, accusations they were not able to prove. Their major concern was that Denny "has simply been talking about his gay [exciting] life in Paris and making them [the other men] discontented."[84] The directors were quite relieved when Denny was reclassified as medically unfit due to a heart murmur and discharged in the spring of 1943.

Like Paul in *Down There on a Visit*, Denny's thinking had changed when he was away at the forestry camp; as he told Christopher as they sat at a bar, "I've decided to hold on to the things I can see."[85]

Denny moved into an apartment above a restaurant on Entrada Drive, close to the beach in Santa Monica, enrolling in the University of California to prepare for his pre-medical examinations, with the hope of becoming a psychiatrist. Both Denny and Christopher realized that Denny had developed new goals and that their days of living together were no longer possible. "Denny is now going along a different road," Christopher wrote in his diary. "His discipline is all built on his studying, which I can't share."[86] As Christopher wrote to Gerald Heard: "Denny has two jobs: one daytime one, as a janitor, during which he studies algebra, Shakespeare and German for his high school diploma, which, in the rush of getting educated in other ways, he never stopped to take—and an evening job at a bookstore [The London Bookstore on Hollywood Boulevard.] We go swimming together every Saturday."[87]

It was here on the beach at Santa Monica that Denny spotted a seagull staggering through the sand. The gull had a broken wing, and touched by its hapless plight, Denny "amputated it, which made the bird more comfortable but didn't solve its problem." Christopher followed it and saw how it couldn't fly, couldn't swim, and was being harassed by other gulls pecking at it. He killed it. "This made me feel horrible all day. I asked Swami, did I do right? and he said no, one shouldn't interfere with the karma of any creature."[88] This didn't convince Christopher, who rationalized that the only other option would have been to take the bird home and make it a pet.

Another day on the beach, Denny made a tail for a kite out of Christmas decorations. ("This sort of play project, undertaken on the spur of the moment, was characteristic of Denny," Christopher noted.)[89] A gust of wind off the ocean caught the kite, it dove, hit a power line by the highway, the tinsel ornaments short-circuited the line, the line sparked, flashed, exploded, fell across the road, cars swerved, brakes squealed, traffic backed up, the neighborhood was without power, the police came, and the kite flyers innocently joined the crowd of spectators. Like everyone else who had lived with him discovered, Denny made life a continuing adventure.

Often, too, they bicycled together. In June, while cycling around Beverly Hills, Denny "suggested we should look in on Lena Horne, the colored singer. She has a little house just above the Sunset Strip. They have become great friends. Denny opened the door and shouted, 'Lena darling, I've brought a friend in to take a shower.' Lena seemed to find this perfectly natural."[90] (While on leave from the forestry camp, Denny and his African-American friends from the camp would "often go down to night spots, in the colored part of town, and Denny is proud of being accepted in places where whites are not welcome.")[91]

On their bicycling trips, Denny started composing a bicycling song to the tune of "Take a Pair Of Sparkling Eyes," a song that began: "Just a pair of cycling queens/no longer in their teens."[92]

Whenever Isherwood went to Santa Monica to visit,

Denny "was very sweet and sympathetic. He suggested, as so often before, that I should come and live with him here, or that we'd go East together and he'd study at Columbia. But I can't walk out on Swami right now. And Denny himself is so unsettled. I could never rely on him."[93] The two were co-dependent, aware of each other's virtues and vices, each appreciative of the strengths of the other and needing them. As Christopher confided to his diary:

> Being with Denny unsettles me, and yet I need him more than ever before ... He's always getting in digs at Swami, whom he's never forgiven, but he doesn't suggest I should leave. His attitude was summed up the other day when he said "either make up your mind to be a monk or a dirty old man." Sometimes I find this kind of brutality bracing; sometimes it just annoys me, because I know, and Denny knows, that he has no right to talk to me like this, when he isn't faced with the same problem himself. If I were to leave [Swami], he'd be pleased in a way, because it would shock a lot of people he dislikes, and because he knows I could only turn to him and depend on him more than ever—most likely we'd live together again. But he'd also be a bit dismayed, I'm sure, because in a strange way he relies on me to do his praying for him; and he would love to be able to believe in my belief.[94]

When they were apart, Christopher had "a gnawing desire to go and see Denny and cry on his shoulder. He's the only person I can discuss the situation with, quite frankly."[95] And then there was always that added benefit, knowing Denny was "waiting at home to cook a tasty evening meal."[96]

So Christopher visited frequently. Tacked to the living room walls of Denny's small, two bedroom and bath apartment were Army posters warning of the dangers of venereal disease. One showed a prostitute with the admonition: "She may be a bag of trouble." The other poster was "a diagram of the penis, with dotted red lines to show the spreading of gonorrheal infection up the urethra and into the bladder."[97] Dominating the wall over the sofa was the huge Picasso that Peter Watson had entrusted to Denny before the War, "Girl Reading at a Table," the portrait of Picasso's twenty-four year old mistress so vividly described in *Down There on a Visit*. The rich colors of this large oil and enamel painting seemed illuminated by the light of the lamp on the table in the painting, with the deep shadows around the girl bending over the table to write giving a sense of quiet concentration to the scene. Denny was well aware of the beauty of this work, and, of its value, and once had stopped Christopher from throwing darts at it (Christopher had slept on the sofa under the painting and had a vivid nightmare about Nazi Germany, which he blamed on the girl in the painting),[98] and had stopped, also, a reveler at one of his parties from slashing it with a broken glass. Christopher noted in his diary that "the frame of the Picasso is a bit more chipped," and speculated "a fight?"[99]

Denny's college career proved short-lived. Ten years older than his fellow freshman, he naturally excelled in his French courses, but the science and math classes he was required to take were beyond him. One of his classmates remembered: "at first he was very serious about his studies, saying that someday he wanted to go on to medical school. But after living adventurously in Europe, he simply couldn't settle into the college routine. He was really too restless, too independent for college and, I think, already too old to change."[100] After a year, he dropped out with vague plans to resume his studies later.

It was not surprising Denny had a hard time concentrating on studying. His apartment had become the headquarters of a continuing party, with young friends coming and going all day and night. Jeff and Curly, who liked pot and porn and who Isherwood believed were capable of blackmail; Wallace and Howard, who lived in another of the upstairs front apartments who were always ready to participate in Denny's schemes; Ken Angermayer who Isherwood described as "a strikingly attractive boy"[101] who would become the acclaimed filmmaker and author of *Hollywood Babylon*, Kenneth Anger.

With Denny the host/circus master, these parties were bound to press the limits. At one, a naval officer and an army lieutenant were persuaded to strip and have sex on the couch under the Picasso as the other guests watched and critiqued.[102] Once, Christopher received a call from George Cukor, the film director, to come to his house at once to speak with Somerset Maugham who at the time was staying there. The author looked up from writing and said in his stammer, "I think, C-Christopher, you'd b-better warn your friend Denham that his apartment is b-being watched by the p-police."[103] Apparently someone had alerted the police that teenage boys were entering and leaving Denny's apartment at all hours. This report of the famed author's warning delighted Denham, for he had bragged that in Europe, before the War, Maugham had been one of his admirers. When not at the apartment, Denny and his friends would drive up the coast to Thelma Todd's, a notorious restaurant—part eating establishment, part casino, part brothel—frequented by Hollywood executives interested in meeting call girls in the establishment's curtained alcoves.

One day Denny came to visit Christopher, bringing two friends with him. Isherwood recalled looking out his window and seeing the three get out of the car and the effect of his first glimpse of one of the young men, Bill Harris, an artist in his early twenties with a shock of blond hair and a swimmer's physique, as "like a shot from an elephant gun" that made him "grunt" with desire. "When Denny and I were alone, I accused him of having maliciously introduced me to this beautiful temptation in order to seduce me away from the Vedanta Center. This was meant as a joke. Nevertheless, I knew that the young man's image had been stamped upon my mind and would reappear at inconvenient moments, in the shrine room and elsewhere. It would be all the more disturbing because I realized already that he himself wasn't unattainable."[104]

On reflection, Christopher believed what he felt for Bill Harris was what he called "a sort of compulsive craze. Bill represented the Forbidden."[105] Isherwood was able to resist this temptation until some weeks later he happened to find himself standing next to Bill, pressed closed together in a crowded trolley car. When Denny took a trip to San Francisco and asked Bill to paint the living room of his apartment while he was gone, Christopher stayed there with Bill and so began their affair. Christopher rationalized his break with the mandates of Vedanta by regarding Bill as "one of the Seven Deadly Sins, which had to be overcome by temporarily yielding to it. 'Let me go to bed with you so I can get tired of you.'"[106]

Looking back, years later, Christopher realized that Denny was a "myth figure" to him.

As he wrote in his diary:

he was Satan, the tempter, the easy-as-an-old-shoe friend who is so comfortable to be with because he knows the worst there is to know about you; the captive audience which holds its entertainers captive, demanding relentlessly to be surprised and amused. Christopher's Satan held Christopher in his power by provoking Christopher to indiscretion. Having dared Christopher to start an affair with someone—"I bet you can't get him," Satan says—he wheedles and flatters Christopher into talking about the new lover. So Christopher finds himself giving a blow-by-blow and word-for-word description of their affair; and thus the affair turns into a theatrical performance.[107]

After Bill Harris moved to New York City, Christopher had an affair with Steve, his studio's mail department messenger boy who was studying to become an actor. Denny rendered his pronouncement on Steve—"I think he's quite beautiful, but let's face it, he'll always be a department store queen"[108]—and set about finding a suitable partner for his friend. Denny introduced him to Bill Caskey, just discharged from the Navy. Denny challenged Christopher to flirt with Caskey and see how far he could get. At a party at Denny's apartment to celebrate Bill's twenty-fourth birthday, Christopher took Bill away from the party to a store in town to buy a shirt for him as a birthday gift and then returned to the party, reporting to Denny that Bill had said he would come to Christopher's home as soon as he left the party. He did and they spent that night together.

Isherwood admired Caskey's outspokenness. At a dinner party at Charlie Chaplin's house, Bill was seated next to Natasha Moffat, the wife of screenwriter Ivan Moffat. When she saw who her seating partner would be, she exclaimed, "Oh good, Billy! I always like sitting next to a pansy." The room grew silent. "Your slang is out of date, Natasha," Bill responded politely and with greater volume, "we can't say 'pansy' nowadays. We say 'cocksucker.'"[109]

To celebrate the end of the War and gas rationing, Christopher in September of 1945 bought a second-hand Lincoln Zephyr convertible, and would roar down the narrow roads of the Hollywood Hills with Denny and Bill in the back seat shrieking, Denny pretending "they were all a bunch of pleasure-mad teenagers of the 1920's, drunk on bathtub gin," and yelling "Let 'er rip!" and "Flaming youth!"[110]

At the end of September, Denny flew to New York City, having had crated and shipped ahead his Picasso; it was time to raise some money and he hoped to interest a dealer in Manhattan in buying the painting. Traveling "by air" was a glamorous but still new adventure, and Denny covered his bases. In his clean script, he wrote on a plain piece of paper:

To whom it may concern:

The picture "Girl Reading" by Picasso which is my property, having been given to me by Peter Watson, is to be the property of Christopher Isherwood in the event of my dying or disappearing before it is sold in consideration of debts I owe to him and because he is my [and here Denny inserted a carrot and added the word "best"] best friend.

He signed it L. Denham Fouts, and dated it September 20, 1945, with the address 137 Entrada Dr. Santa Monica beneath the date, and at the bottom of the page a line which read:

Witness: and signed by William E. Caskey[111]

In New York, Denny sold the Picasso to a man he met at a cocktail party who offered more for the painting, $9,500, than any of the dealers he had approached. (That buyer in turn sold it to Mr. and Mrs. Samuel Marx of Chicago. It was Mrs. Marx—Florence May Schoenborg—heiress to the May Department Store chain fortune, who was an avid collector of modern art, and who, at her death in 1995, willed this painting, and a collection of others, to the Metropolitan Museum of Art where it hangs today as part of the permanent exhibit, a single painting from the collection Peter Watson had assembled, worth today well over fifty million dollars.)

When Denny returned from New York to California in the spring of 1946, Christopher and Bill were living in his apartment. Denny stayed with them, but it wasn't long before

Denny and Bill were quarrelling. Christopher believed Denny was jealous when he realized that his best friend and Bill were truly in love, that he had lost Christopher. Denny told Christopher that Bill was "just another boy, another pawn in the sexual chess game."[112] Christopher in his diary analyzed what happened:

> And now Denny, that sly old chess player, had made a crude amateur mistake; he had challenged Caskey from a position of weakness. Caskey saw his advantage and pushed their quarrel to the point at which Christopher had to choose between them. Thus it was that Christopher's friendship with Denny ended. Christopher was sorry, of course. Denny may have been sorry, too—yes, I'm sure he was. But he accepted the situation with his usual arrogant show of indifference. He was in one of his self-destructive moods, ready to break with anyone who wouldn't submit to his will. Christopher, who was also capable of such moods, understood this perfectly. Though he had sided with Caskey, his sympathies remained with Denny. Looking back on the two relationships, it seems to me that Christopher and Denny came closer to each other than Christopher and Caskey ever did.[113]

Denny left the apartment, subletting it, went back East with Trotsky and from there to Europe.

Over three decades later, thinking about Denny, Christopher would reflect: "I *liked* Denny. He was witty, he could make me laugh, and he could instruct me how to live in this country ... And for all his reservations and sneerings about religion, he did take Vedanta seriously. He resisted it, he attacked it, he hated it: but he knew it wasn't merely silly, a freaky game. He was a curiously serious person, despite his air of frivolity."[114]

In *Down There on a Visit*, Isherwood expressed best his feelings about his friend: "I never in my life met anyone who was so much fun to be with ... He had a genius for enjoying himself."[115]

CHAPTER SIX

"A MARVELOUS SOUTHERN WHORE NAMED DENHAM FOUTS"

The Europe that Denny found when he had returned in the spring of 1946 was very different from the world he left in June of 1940 when Peter sent him to the United States for the duration.

What had become of his European friends during those horrific years?

Lord Tredegar's wife had died in 1937. Evan did have a knack for marrying well. In Singapore on March 13, 1939, forty-six-year-old Evan married twenty-four-year-old Princess Olga Sergeievna Dolgorousky from a family of Russian nobility that, before the Revolution, had been close to the Imperial family. The couple divorced four years later; it appeared to have been a rather unhappy marriage that included an incident in which Evan tried to set fire to his wife.[1]

Through his family's standing, Evan found himself at the outset of the War just where he didn't belong: in MI5, Britain's esteemed counter-intelligence agency. Thinking well outside the box, his first scheme was to have peregrine falcons, like the ones he had trained at Tredegar Park to entertain the guests at his garden parties, attack German carrier pigeons and thereby disrupt the flow of classified information to pre-invasion agents. It was never clear just how the falcons would distinguish enemy pigeons from neutral pigeons or develop a taste for Nazi pigeons more than other avian delicacies flying the skies at the same time. This scheme morphed into a plan to slow the German push into France and Belgium by letting loose a massive flock of pigeons that would mingle with the Nazi carrier pigeons and confuse the Germans as to which pigeons were theirs. The RAF gave it a try with a squadron of planes taking off with cargo holds full of thousands of pigeons. Over the southern coast of England, the pigeons dropped from the planes were instantly killed by the intake of the engines. Evan refined his plan. The next time the pigeons were taken aloft, they were in individual brown paper bags, the bags were let loose over the coast, and by the time the pigeons burst from the bags they at least were free of the planes; but rather than traveling to mingle with their fascist counterparts, they made their way immediately back home to their familiar roosts.

Despite these setbacks, Evan was quite proud of his work as commander of the Falcon Interceptor Unit of MI5, and one day, as he lunched with Lady Baden-Powell, broke all edicts of the counter-intelligence agency by showing her around his office and describing in detail the war efforts in which he was involved. This was a blatant violation of the oath of secrecy he had taken, and Evan at once was arrested and imprisoned in the Tower of London. In due course, he was freed, and, fuming, made his way back to Tredegar Park.

Evan was not about to let the matter pass. He knew just who to contact to plan suitable revenge against those who summarily had imprisoned him: the infamous sixty-eight-year-old Aleister Crowley, a character the British tabloids had dubbed the "Beast of the Apocalypse," the "King of Depravity," the "Wickedest Man on Earth."

Crowley, who fancied himself, with Shakespeare, one of the two greatest poets of the English language, held himself out as a prophet of a new era that would supplant Christianity, an era when men would become gods. The central credo of his ministry was "Do what thou wilt shall be the whole of the law," a credo that focused on individual freedom while flirting with license and anarchy. A mystic, a spiritual philosopher who fiddled with the concept of reality, Crowley considered magick (as he spelled it to distinguish it from pedestrian tricks of magic) "the science and art of causing change in conformity with will."[2] His rituals and sacraments, in which genital secretions served the same role as the wine and wafer, included the use of hashish, mescaline, heroin, and opium, sexual magick with both male and female partners, and the consumption of the blood of cats.

Crowley was a student of occultism, and his devotion to magick and mysticism paralleled Evan's, who before the War had been a member of the "Black Hand," a private occult society in London, and who recently had been constructing, at great cost, an elaborate magick temple on his estate. Surely here was just the person to help perform a little black magick to bring about the revenge against his arresting officer that Evan craved. The two conspirators were kindred spirits. Crowley had been a guest at many of Evan's notorious weekend parties and had inscribed one of his books, *The Book of Thoth*, to Evan as follows: "To my old and very dear Friend and Colleague, Adept of Adepts in the Secret Tradition, Eifon Morgan, heir of the Mysteries of the Round Table, entitled to bear Excalibur, Lord of the Secret Marches about Camelot do I, being the pupil and heir of Merlin, entrust this Book, Aleister Crowley."[3]

So Evan was well aware of just what havoc Crowley could wreak when on May 18, 1943, he wrote to the Great Beast, inviting him to come stay at Tredegar Park. Crowley arrived on June 17, and was housed in the Oak Room, the grandest in the mansion, a forty-two-foot long bedroom that once had been the main state dining room of Tredegar House, with its massive fireplace and seventeenth century oak paneling carved with busts of the Roman emperors, scrolls of acanthus leaves, and grotesque heads. On Sunday, June 20, 1943, Crowley wrote in his diary: "Saw T's Magick room— far greater than I thought."[4] That was saying something.

Crowley stayed at Tredegar Park for two weeks to carry out his work. Exactly what sort of black magick the two concocted, what spells cast, what séances conducted, is not known, though the conspirators were suitably smug when, soon after the Great Beast's visit, they learned that the officer who had had Evan thrown into the Tower of London was beset with a painful illness that brought him satisfyingly close to death.

And what during the War had become of Prince Paul of Greece with whom Denny had sailed the Aegean, and who shared with Denny an identical tattoo over his heart?

Crown Princess Federica, who had wed Prince Paul in January of 1938, dutifully gave birth to their first child, a daughter, in November of that year, and a son two years later. That was to be just about the only happiness the couple shared for the next six years. The Third Reich tried to convince Paul's brother, King George II of Greece, to abdicate in favor of Prince Paul, who had married a German princess and who, therefore, the Reich assumed, would be more sympathetic to Germany than the King; a promise of protection from Mussolini's Italy came with this overture. The King and Crown Prince would have nothing of it, and Italy invaded Greece on October 28, 1940, followed by the German army attacking across the Bulgarian border. The Greek government retreated to the island of Crete and then, when Crete was bombed, took refuge in Cairo, where the Crown Prince stayed, and London, where the King set up government in Claridge's hotel. After three years of exile, the Monarchy with the British army invaded Greece to take it back. The country was freed by November of 1944 and the King and Prince Paul returned to

Athens. With the death of King George, Prince Paul would ascend to the throne on April 1, 1947.

And Peter Watson? During the War, he lived by himself in a modest flat in Palace Gate in London, and volunteered as a clerk for the Red Cross, driving a Red Cross van. Accustomed to traveling the world, he was confined to England, never his favorite country, and after a while began to go stir crazy. He wrote to a friend on January 11, 1943 that "the whole thing [the War] has been going on much too long I feel, and ... it is very depressing for me to have lost all sense of contact with Denham ... After four years the sense of tension is unbearable."[5] Taxes were rising in England during the War years, and the income Peter received from the trusts his father had established was falling. He was still supporting young artists and authors, but his days of Bentleys and Vuitton luggage were in the past. Even worse, some of his investments, and all of his art collection, were in German-occupied France. He had lost contact with Sherban Sidery, the Rumanian caretaker he had left in charge of his apartment, and worried about whether the caretaker had been able to protect the paintings or whether the Nazis had found and confiscated the collection. Peter was fatalistic about the dangers of the day: "There is even a great jagged hole in the Ritz," he wrote to Cecil Beaton, "but so far this block has escaped. I never go to a shelter—I would rather die in my sleep."[6]

As the War dragged on, Peter had become philosophical, too, about his art collection far away in his apartment in Paris. "I had an International Red Cross message from the Rumanian Sidery who has stayed in my flat," he wrote to Cecil Beaton; "A good thing really I feel to have someone in the flat. The pictures I am afraid have gone—a pity really because I had attempted to get the most interesting work of any painter I ever bought and it was all most deliberately chosen. But I don't care as it seems to be fatal to one's character to attach oneself too much to things."[7]

Peter was therefore to some extent, mentally prepared for what he found when he and Cyril Connolly at last got back to his apartment in Paris and found the rooms in shambles, the entire art collection gone, and, scattered around the apartment, tell-tale pawn tickets: his caretaker, the man he had left in charge, was responsible for the loss of the paintings, the gold knives and forks, everything of value. All of this Peter could accept. The apartment could be cleaned and renovated for Denny's homecoming. What Peter did not expect, and could not accept, was how Denny so quickly "lapsed into a sort of pre-war cocktail haute pederast life."[8]

A few days after passing out on the bathroom floor where Michael Wishart and Jean Connolly had found him with the heroin needle hanging from his arm, Denny had himself admitted to a clinic. Faithful Peter wired money to cover the expense of his treatment and the around-the-clock nurses who would be necessary for some days after the treatment.

Denny emerged from the clinic with two black eyes, the result of electric shock treatments, and a surly mood. Michael, who at the same time had given up opium on his own and was trying to ease the transition with alcohol and barbiturates, was equally disagreeable.

Peter telephoned and suggested that the two take some time to go to the country to relax and enjoy the fresh air. He paid for their stay at Moret in a hotel that overlooked the River Loing.

It was late autumn, with mists over the river and leaves of gold, and Denny and Michael savored the good food at the hotel and the exhilaration of riding horses through the forests. It seemed as if they had regained their Eden, this time a healthier one. "The weeks I am describing were so intensely happy," Michael remembered, that I would not for anything have interrupted their pure joy wondering what was to become of our more than friendship on return to Paris. It is the privilege of the young, and of the stupid, to give no thought to the morrow."[9]

On one of their excursions, the two went to the Chateau de Fontainebleau, where Michael wanted to paint the ancient carp that had been swimming the garden pools since the days of King Louis XIV. While walking around the chateau, Denny dropped a gold pill box. Its white powder contents spilled on the cobblestones: heroin. Michael realized at once how completely Denny's addiction had consumed him—"it requires great cunning to conceal a heroin habit from someone with whom one is living intimately."[10] The two returned to Paris to Peter's flat at 44 Rue du Bac and even before the luggage was unpacked, Denny had taken out his opium pipe from its hiding place behind one of the wall panels, and "smoked furiously" as if to make up for lost time.[11]

Another year of all this was quite enough. In March of 1947, Peter returned to Paris to remove everything from his flat so that he could terminate the lease. He was concerned about this mission, both because he was never sure if, in the presence of Denny, his determination would falter, and because he would have to tell Denny about his own new affair. Ten days before he was to leave New York to return to England, Peter had been invited to a dinner party. There he met Waldemar Hansen, a twenty-four-year-old aspiring poet who had the clean, crew-cut look of an American college student and who was fascinated by literature and art. Hansen later remembered that evening: "Peter had a wonderfully engaging way about him, a winsome way of smiling, a way of making people feel that he was absolutely on their wavelength. Early in our first evening together it was quite clear that something was transpiring between us. In the course of dinner we had both fallen quite silent, with [the host] doing all the talking, and Peter was simply looking at me mutely, and I was looking back at him. It really was love at first sight. Suffice it to say that Peter stayed the night."[12] Peter asked him to come live with him in London, though Waldemar was reluctant to leave his friends and family. "Then come stay with me at least for the summer," Watson pressed. "If you do only that, I will give you a summer that you will never forget."[13] Waldemar agreed and would join Peter in London later in April.

It was time for Peter to tell Denny it was over. As he wrote to Waldemar, "I am rather worried about his reactions as I must tell him everything, and he is still more attached to me than to anyone else and is likely to stay so." Predictably, Denny was devastated, whether because of losing Peter's love, or losing Peter's financial support. "Poor Denham," Watson updated Hansen:

The situation is tragic. He senses that the worst for him has happened as I told him that I really cared about you. I have plenty of guilt about him, although it is not justified. I cannot love people I do not really respect, and I cannot respect the life he leads here. He still loves me, probably more than ever now since I have gone beyond his reach, and I suppose he will until we have been completely separated for a year or so, which must happen I think now.[14]

Over the course of three weeks, Watson had his furnishings crated and removed from the apartment, so that all that was left were six Venetian shell chairs, and in Denny's bedroom the massive bed, the Tchleitchev painting, and the red-shaded lamp. Even then, Denny did not believe that Peter would carry through on his threat to terminate his lease. Peter did. Denny refused to leave. The landlord lost no time taking the matter to court to have his troublesome tenant evicted, but month after month the matter remained mired on the court's docket.

With Denny's heroin addiction came a consuming paranoia. He paid men to buy drugs for him, which of course led to extortion and the receipt of diluted drugs. In his eyes, everyone was an informant and he was sure the police were trying to trap him. An unexpected knock on the apartment door would cause him almost to faint, and he only answered if he heard the correct code of knocks. He realized that the fact that he was with teenagers as young as Gerard and Michael further increased his exposure to arrest.

Yet even as his troubles grew, so did his reputation, and celebrants continued to come to meet the legend in person. Tony Watson-Gandy, a British Royal Air Force officer during the War, had joined Michael and Gerard as Denny's latest live-in worshipper, taking up residence in Peter's apartment. And a stream of visitors arrived at 44 Rue du Bac for a chance to meet the famous Denham Fouts. Among them came twenty-two-year-old Gore Vidal to observe this curiosity in his habitat.

In the preceding decade, Eugene Luther Gore Vidal, Jr., had transformed himself into Gore Vidal: young literary lion.

Ten years before, into Gore's rather lonely and unhappy adolescence dominated by a hard drinking, caustic, unpredictable mother he detested, who divorced his father when Gore was ten, (and whose periods, he later wryly commented, had been "more excruciating than those of any other woman in medical history")[15], into the gray Gothic world of St. Albans in Washington, D.C., where his mother sent him as a boarding student, a school where bullies would stampede a student into a locker, lock it, and leave, into this world of adolescent uncertainty and fear had walked a schoolboy god "and the first human happiness that I had ever encountered."[16]

It was the winter of 1937, mid-term, when twelve-year-old Jimmie Trimble started at St. Albans. Gore checked out Jimmie's pubic hair in the communal shower—"bright gold curls"—and "as I looked at him, he gave me a big grin and so it began, likeness drawn to likeness, soon to be made whole by desire minus the obligatory pursuit."[17] In class, "Jimmie and I would signal each other when a hard-on had arrived unbidden."[18]

Gore's mother was relieved when on occasion her son

93

brought his new friend home for a weekend visit to "Merrywood," Gore's step-father's Georgian mansion set on forty acres above the Potomac River in McLean, Virginia, with tennis court, squash court, swimming pool, and woods, delighted that at last her bookish son, who spent all his time reading, had any friend. It was at Merrywood, on the white tile floor of a bathroom out of view of the butler, that "there we were, belly to belly, in the act of becoming one," where "we simply came together."[19]

Jimmie would become the golden boy of St. Albans. He was captain of the basketball team, a star of the football team, and a legend of the baseball team, the ace pitcher who strung together a record of no-hitters with his fastballs and curve balls, thrown at such speed that the catcher had to get extra padding for his glove. Jimmie was handsome at twelve, a grown-up, according to Vidal, at fourteen, downright striking at seventeen. There he is in a photograph at seventeen looking remarkably contemporary in a light-colored boat-neck sweater, no shirt underneath. Is he aware how perfectly that sweater set off his chest and broad shoulders? The thrust of his athlete's neck? The square jaw? The knowing grin, that smile like Gatsby's "with a quality of eternal reassurance in it," that smile that, according to another friend, "would just knock the birds out of the trees,"[20] those blue eyes that seemed to look at the humorous side of life, that seemed to intimate that he saw right into everyone? The wavy blond hair? "Did you ever tell a man that he was *beautiful*?"[21] a shocked Jimmie asked his mother after a girlfriend had used that word to describe him. He exuded a definite sexual energy, a masculine magnetism that pulled everyone into his world. He was like Phineas of John Knowles' *A Separate Peace*, with no one immune from his pull. A retired English master from St. Albans who had taught there when Jimmie Trimble was a student recalled that Jimmie "usually, at 17, moved through the Lane Johnston halls briskly, but when he idled along, he had a generous roll of the hips—the flexible hips of the athlete—that promised, like the Anglican definition of faith—'the substance of things hoped for, the evidence of things unseen.' But I was too much the unsure 27 year-old master to do more than cast my eyes demurely down, probably not too far down, as he passed by."[22] Clearly when Jimmie walked by, there were masters and students, male and female admirers, silently staring.

Late spring, 1939. Before leaving for a school trip to France, Gore remembered, "Jimmie and I made love in the woods above the roaring river. I remember his almost-mature body with the squared bony shoulders and rosy skin against bright green ... After sex, we swam against the swift, deadly current of the forbidden Potomac River, swam among rocks and driftwood to a special large gray-brown glacial rock, where we lay, side by side. We're going to go on doing this for the rest of our lives, I remember thinking, tempting—no, driving—fate to break us in two ... Every now and then, in idle moments, I start to hear snatches of the conversation of those two boys on the rock that afternoon," on that "cloudless sunny day when Europe was ahead of me and all I cared for beside me."[23]

After the summer, Gore was sent to Los Alamos Ranch School in New Mexico, and the following year to Exeter in New Hampshire, while Jimmie stayed at St. Albans.

The next time, and the last time, Gore saw Jimmie was during the 1942 Christmas season when the two met at the holiday dance of Mrs. Shippen's Dancing School. "We had last seen each other as fourteen year-old boys. Now we were seventeen year-old men. Would we take up where we had left off in the spring of 1939 on a May day, in the woods above the Potomac River?"[24] It was an awkward reunion when they spotted each other in their tuxedos in the ballroom with their dates. Gore had known his date Rosalind for several years, and the two just had announced that they would marry after Gore graduated from Exeter in June, before his enlistment in the

Army in July. Gore told Jimmie of his marriage plans. "You're crazy", Jimmie said, as the two of them left their dates and walked downstairs to the men's room. " ...[O]ur bodies still fitted perfectly together, as we promptly discovered inside one of the cubicles, standing up, belly to belly, talking of girls and marriage and coming simultaneously."[25]

Jimmie's pitching prowess had caught the attention of the owner of the Washington Senators who gave him a signing bonus and a four year scholarship to Duke University. Early in 1944, as soon as he turned eighteen and no longer needed the consent of his mother, Jimmie enlisted in the Marine Corps. He and his girlfriend, Christine White, voted the "prettiest blonde" at her school, agreed to marry when Jimmie returned from service. In July of 1944, Trimble joined the Third Marine Division in the South Pacific, and Vidal enlisted in the Army and found himself on a ship in the Aleutians.

After serving for several months on Guam where he was the star pitcher for the Third Marine Division's baseball team, Trimble volunteered to join a scouting platoon for the landing on Iwo Jima. The stark statistics bespeak the horror of those bloody days. Twenty-two thousand Japanese defended the four mile island. It would take the American forces over a month to control the island at a cost of seven thousand dead and more than twenty thousand wounded, with all but one thousand Japanese soldiers dead.

Eight days after the first landing, Jimmie volunteered to join a reconnaissance team trying to pinpoint the location of rocket sites so that artillery could be called in to take them out. In a midnight attack on his team's fox hole, a Japanese soldier with a mine strapped to him jumped in and wrapped himself around Jimmie, blowing both of them to death.

That spring, the Marine's Third Division baseball field on Guam was officially dedicated as Trimble Field, a story reported in all the Washington, D.C., newspapers. There was a memorial service held in the Washington Cathedral where

Jimmie lay in state. "I can't think of how a nineteen year-old Marine private would merit a 'state' burial," Vidal wondered years later, "but on the other hand, he was much loved by Washington sports fans."[26] One of Jimmie's St. Albans teammates went into shock when he learned of Jimmie's death, was treated for acute depression, and had to leave college. Christine White, the girl Jimmie had known for three months before he went overseas and who later became a television actress starring in movies and appearing in television series like *Bonanza*, *The Fugitive*, and *Perry Mason*, stayed in touch with Jimmie's mother for decades. She kept his letters and photographs all those years and showed Gore Vidal a snapshot of herself that had been in Jimmie's wallet when he was killed. Laying it, curled and rounded, on the table as she and Vidal dined fifty years after the War, she explained that "It still follows the shape of his body." Vidal could see. "There," he noted, "on the dining room table in Willard's Hotel, was the outline of the curve made by Jimmie's buttock."[27] During the fiftieth reunion of Vidal's class at St. Albans, one of the members of the class went to visit another who was institutionalized. When he mentioned Jimmie, Ted, ("whom Jimmie had bedded") "sat up straight, and said, 'Why, he was just here. He just now left. If you hurry, you can find him in the hall.'"[28] Such was Jimmie Trimble's hold on the imaginations of those who had known him.

As for Gore Vidal, from that day he last saw him "and left Jimmie to time and chance,"[29] his world never again was the same. He would think of him the rest of his life. Hanging on the wall beside his bed was a life-size reproduction of a portrait of Jimmie as a teenager. Now and then, Jimmie would appear to him in visions, as "completely present, as he had been in the bedroom of Merrywood": Jimmie "opened his blue eyes and smiled and yawned and put his hand alongside my neck."[30] And "for years, whenever I was in a numinous place

97

like Delphi or Delos, I would address the night: Jimmie, are you anywhere? And almost always the wind would rise."[31] Late in his life, Vidal bought a small plot in Rock Creek Park Cemetery in Washington, D.C., just a few yards from where Jimmie Trimble lay in the shade of a copper beech. "Was there ever so furious and restless a ghost?" Gore Vidal asks in his memoirs, "or is it that we, the survivors, are so traumatized to this day by his abrupt absence from our lives that we are still trying to summon his ghost?"[32]

Looking back from the vantage point of his seventh decade, Vidal realized that when he knew Jimmie Trimble, he was whole "for what proved to be the last time ...I not only never again encountered the other half, but by the time I was twenty-five, I had given up all pursuit, settling for a thousand brief anonymous adhesions ... Quite enough, I think if the real thing has happened."[33]

"I am neither a believer in an afterlife nor a mystic," Vidal wrote further in his memoirs, "and unlike Santayana, I cannot begin to imagine what it must be like. Yet I still want Jimmie to *be*, somewhere, if only on this page."[34] And indeed he was. Jimmie appears time and again, in one guise or another, in many of Vidal's novels, *The Season of Comfort, Washington, D.C., Two Sisters, The City and the Pillar, The Judgment of Paris, The Smithsonian Institution*, and throughout his memoir *Palimpsest*.

Vidal's emergence as a prominent author had been all but instantaneous. He graduated from Exeter in June of 1943, entered the Enlisted Reserve Corps of the Army the next month, became the first mate of an army supply ship in the Aleutians, and on his night watches began drafting in pencil in an accounts book his first novel. He completed his book nine months later. *Williwaw*—an Eskimo term for the violent storms that bore down on the Bering Sea—was based on his own military experience in the Aleutians, published in 1946 by Dutton, and hailed as one of the first war novels, and by a nineteen year old author, no less. Vidal immediately assumed a place among those perceived as the next generation of American literary lions.

"With the finishing of this book, my life as a writer began."[35] Books tumbled out of him. The next year, he published *In a Yellow Wood*, a coming-of-age novel in which the main character had to choose between a predictable life and an unconventional lifestyle, perhaps reflecting the tensions Vidal was feeling between the pull of a political life—following in the path of his grandfather Senator Thomas Gore—or a more bohemian, literary life. ("I ... was brought up by a politician grandfather in Washington, D.C. and I wanted very much to be a politician, too. Unfortunately, nature had designed me to be a writer. I had no choice in the matter.")[36] Whatever its origins, it was a minor book Vidal later in his life would call his "worst novel."[37]

His next more than made up for this lackluster performance. Published less than a year later, on January 10, 1948, *The City and the Pillar* was dedicated "For the memory of J.T.", and was, as Vidal described it, a novel in which he described what might have happened had he and Jimmie met again after the War. Vidal knew he was moving into uncharted, dangerous territory with this book. "I knew that my description of the love affair between two normal all-American boys of the sort that I had spent three years with in the wartime army would challenge every superstition about sex in my native land."[38] After he read the new novel, Orville Prescott, the influential book reviewer for the *New York Times*, told Vidal's editor that he would never again read, much less review, a book by Vidal. The *Times* refused to advertise it, as did all major newspapers and magazines. "In freedom's land," Vidal wrote years later in describing the shock caused by his new novel, "what ought not to be is not and must be blacked out."[39] But within two weeks of publication, *The City and the Pillar* was riding the *New York Times* best seller list along with Truman Capote's *Other Voices,*

Other Rooms and Norman Mailer's *The Naked and the Dead*, and a triumphant twenty-two-year-old Vidal was off to Rome.

There, at a dinner party in February, he met and befriended the famed thirty-seven-year-old playwright, Tennessee Williams, whose *A Streetcar Named Desire* was then a national sensation and a year later would win a Pulitzer Prize. The two traveled around Italy in an old Jeep that Tennessee had bought, and Gore remembered never laughing so much with anyone in his life.

From Rome, the two friends in April drove to Paris where "there were Bellow and Mailer and Capote and Baldwin and Bowles, while Tennessee and I shared a floor of the small Hotel de L'Universite".[40]

This amazing assemblage of young authors eager to experience Europe after the War was soon augmented by the arrival of Christopher Isherwood, who, with Bill Caskey, landed at Le Havre on April 22. They immediately made their way to Paris, past the many reminders of the War—"small military graveyards, smashed houses, provisional half-rebuilt bridges over which the train moved cautiously"—straight to the Rue du Bac to Peter Watson's flat to see Denny.[41]

It was a Saturday evening, April 24, 1948. Christopher recorded his thoughts in his diary:

> It is a huge shabby place with traces of the splendor of his pre-1939 period, in which he leads a nocturnal Proustian life with the tattered curtains always drawn. He lies most of the day in bed, with Trotsky and the pipe at his side, reading and dozing, often eating nothing but a plate of cooked cereal. When he can't afford opium, he drinks a kind of tea made of the dross, which gives him stomach cramps. He is as pale as a corpse, but quite unchanged, slim as ever, and a sort of waxen beauty. He did not seem at all vague or stupefied, as [Bill] Harris had told us and he

welcomed us both warmly. He is liable to be thrown out of the apartment before long, and doesn't know where he'll go.[42]

Denny introduced Isherwood and Caskey to some young French friends who were there that evening. Writing in another diary entry thirty years later, Isherwood described the scene: "They began what sounded like a parody of Frenchified intellectual conversation. One of them made a sneering reference to those dupes who believe in a life after death. What I can still hear as I write this [three decades later] is the withering tone in which Denny silenced him, exclaiming, 'You little *fool!*' Denny's scorn was quite uncannily impressive. It was as if he *knew*."[43]

The next day, Isherwood and Caskey were sitting in the Café les Deux Magots when Gore Vidal walked by, recognized Isherwood, and stopped to introduce himself. Earlier in the year, Vidal had sent him an advance copy of *The City and the Pillar* seeking an endorsement, and the famed author had praised it. When he sat down to talk, Gore asked Christopher advice on how to manage his writing career, and the two struck up a friendship that would last for years, each appreciating the other's sense of humor. (Both later admitted that in this first encounter, each felt the other was flirting, but neither made the first move, then or ever.)

The next evening and the next, Isherwood, Caskey, and Vidal dined together. It was that second evening that this group joined up with John Lehmann, Isherwood's publisher; through Isherwood's introduction, Vidal had engaged Lehmann as his English publisher. As Vidal described him, he had "a tiger's grin, liked to call people Ducky" and "sexually, it was his pleasure to beat working-class boys; otherwise, he lived a life of perfect domestic virtue ..."[44]

After dinner, the friends took Vidal to 44 Rue du Bac to visit Denny, into that room with the great bed and the "magnificent Tchelitchev painting hanging over it."[45]

Vidal noted that "Denham's legendary beauty was not visible to me."[46] This may have been because Denny was the anti-Jimmie. If Jimmie was the all-American boy next door, then Denny was a walking orgasm. Gore saw Denny as "very pale, with dark lank Indian hair and blank dark eyes, usually half shut: ... He was slender and boyish, with a markedly asymmetrical face."[47]

Gore sat on the side of Denny's bed with John Lehmann, with Trotsky sprawled on the other side. Denny went through his ritualistic ceremony of preparing his opium pipe, "inhaled deeply and exhaled slowly blue medicinal-smelling smoke."[48] Trotsky greedily inhaled the smoke.

"Here," he said to Gore, handing him the long opium pipe.

Gore protested that he couldn't even inhale cigarette smoke, but, good guest that he was, gave it a try, had a "coughing fit" and was "deathly ill."[49] Other than politely offering his visitors a chance to smoke, Denny never pressed anyone to keep trying. As Isherwood remembered the evening, "he let us all take puffs at the pipe, scolding us for our awkwardness and saying we should never make real smokers. It tasted like incense and had no apparent effect whatsoever."[50] As the others watched, Denny continued his ritual, his eyes half shut, then closed, and then, after a while, began to speak, his lulling voice now a run-on jumble of a monologue of people and places and thoughts:

"Cyril was just here. His first trip to Paris since the war. Peter and I took him to a restaurant down the street where he ordered a huge lunch—he's very fat and greedy, you know—and he ate it all up very fast and then he ordered a second lunch and ate that, too. Then he fainted. The waiters carried him back here and put him over there on the floor. I want to meet Truman Capote. I have his picture here."[51]

The *Life* magazine with the famous photograph of the

young Capote rested under one of Denny's opium pipes. Gore told Denny he was sure they would get along.

Denny continued: "I've just had a telegram from Prince Paul—only he's King Paul now. We lived together—well, traveled a lot together before the war, but then he had to get married to Frederika and so we stopped seeing each other because I was living in Santa Monica by then anyway and working in that bookshop and seeing Chris and Gerald . . ."[52]

Fascinated by what he was hearing, Gore was skeptical. Were all the names, all these stories, a result of the opium haze? As he soon learned, Denham never had to fabricate or embellish.

It was a few days later, on April 29, when the group met Denny for cocktails at the Ritz. Isherwood described Denny as looking like "Dorian Gray emerging from the tomb—death-pale and very slim in his dark elegant suit, with black hat and umbrella. He looks like the Necropolitan ambassador."[53] After he sat down, Denny asked Bill Caskey to take some money and get a package of opium from a "connection" who was waiting outside the restaurant. Isherwood thought this request outrageous and refused to let Caskey go, afraid the police could be watching the pusher and that Caskey would be arrested. He felt that Denny's suggestion "was an entirely characteristic act of aggression."[54] (After Christopher left Paris at the end of April, Denny sent him a letter: "I hope you and Billy will go on being as happy as you seem to be." Isherwood noted that "Denny obviously didn't hope it.")[55]

Isherwood found that Denny seemed to be quite himself, not in the least "depressed or debauched or down-at-hell." But his stomach cramps may have been acting up that evening for he merely picked at the caviar and watched the others eat "with an air of controlled distaste, as though our addiction to solid food were a far more squalid vice than his. Now and then, his manner became a trifle vague, but his wit was as sharp as ever."[56]

(This dinner found its way into "Paul," Isherwood's chapter about Denny in *Down There on a Visit*. In "Paul,"

Christopher, the narrator, goes to visit Paul in Paris at his apartment on the Rue du Bac. Propped up in bed, "he was corpse-white, and his face looked as though it had the firmness of hard wax and was semitransparent. There was an air about him of being somehow preserved and, at the same time, purified: his skin seemed to be absolutely without blemish. Indeed, he was marvelously, uncannily beautiful. He wore a heavy skiing sweater over pajamas. Gigi lay on the bed at his feet."[57] Paul told Christopher that he used opium and said, "I hear you've been working in the movies a lot lately, so perhaps you can give me some money?" Paul proposed that they go for dinner at The Ritz. "The Paul who appeared that evening had a sinister, sepulchral elegance; Dorian Gray arisen from the tomb. He wore a perfectly tailored black suit with a black hat and a neatly rolled umbrella. Gigi was at his heels." He ate only caviar. Again, he asked Christopher for money to buy opium, and Christopher gave him thirty thousand francs.)[58]

Gore had read in that day's paper that King Paul of Greece had pneumonia, and as the evening wore down, he mentioned this to Denny.

"I must send him a telegram," Denny said, and together, Gore and Denny located on St. Germain a Western Union office still open and Denny sent the telegram.

The day after the telegram was sent, Denny showed Gore the reply telegram he received from King Paul:

"Darling Denham, so wonderful to hear from you.
Why haven't I heard from you before? Much
exaggerated about my illness ... Love, Paul."[59]

Gore realized at that moment that all of Denny's stories were true.

By then, Vidal was visiting Denny regularly. (Isherwood wrote in his memoirs that "Denny treats Gore with the slightly sarcastic tolerance of an elder uncle."[60]) "At sundown," Vidal recalled, "like Dracula, Denham would appear in the streets leading his dog down St.-Germain-des-Prés."[61] Here, certainly, was a character in search of an author, and Vidal, consciously or not, filed in his memory-bank his encounters with Denny. It was not long, just two years, before Denny appeared in his fiction.

It was in the summer of 1950 when Vidal was twenty-four. He had just bought "Edgewater," a Greek revival mansion on the Hudson River in Dutchess County, New York, ninety miles from New York City, a home that has often been regarded as one of the most beautiful in the United States. It was built in 1820 for a member of the Livingston family, a Palladian villa with a monumental classical portico of six massive two-story Doric columns on the river side, and a lawn that rolled one-hundred-fifty feet down to ancient weeping willows which lined the water's edge. The home had its drawbacks. The mansion had been deserted for years and needed every imaginable repair, its lawns had grown waist high, and worst of all, the New York Central's railroad tracks ran twenty-five yards behind the house, with trains rumbling by each hour. But the River was a mile wide there and the sound of the wind waves drifted through the open French doors, and the views of the Catskill Mountains, purple in the distance, were magical. With a ten thousand dollar mortgage and six thousand dollars borrowed from family members, it was his, and Gore moved in in July of 1950.

The book he wrote in the soaring twenty-six foot high octagonal library at Edgewater was *The Judgment of Paris*, a book he always regarded as one of his favorites and sometimes called his best book, "the novel in which I found my own voice."[62] This picaresque novel centers on the wanderings of Philip Warren, a twenty-eight-year-old American, a graduate of Harvard Law School, who travels around Italy, France, and Egypt after the Second World War, just as Vidal visited Rome, Paris, and Cairo in 1948 and 1949. One of the characters Philip encounters in Paris is Jim. Vidal later confirmed that this Jim was the same Jim Willard from *The City and the Pillar*, who was based on Jimmie Trimble, only now Jimmie had morphed into Denny. "High romantics who fall from the heights make very good drug addicts. I suppose, unconsciously, I was grafting onto him   ...some characteristics of a marvelous southern whore named Denham Fouts."[63]

How close to the mark was Vidal's portrayal of Denny as Jim in *The Judgment of Paris*? Who better to assess his accuracy than Denny's friend, Michael Wishart, who characterized as "brilliant" Vidal's vignette of Denham, with Denny appearing in the novel "very much in character."[64] As Vidal sat on the side of Denny's bed, as he dined with him, the young author was exploring the thoughts of so strange a character, gathering material, and the essence of their conversations found their way into this novel.

In *The Judgment of Paris*, Philip Warren when in Paris meets Jim, with his "low Southern voice" and "slow engaging smile," and, dressed "like a conservative schoolboy in dark grey trousers and a sports coat," just as Denny dressed. Vidal gives this character "golden hair and dark blue eyes," essentially fusing Jimmie Trimble's physical characteristics onto Denny. Jim invites Philip to join him the next evening at an outdoor café. They meet, and in a coming storm, Jim takes Philip to his apartment where the bedroom is very much like Denny's with "a large carved bed of dark wood with four posters" in the center of the room and on the mantle "unframed drawings of Tchelichew and Picasso," and outside the window, the same courtyard where Michael Wishart heard the rain on the gravel when he awoke with Denny.

Gathering through their conversation the nature of Jim's profession, Philip, curious, begins inquiring about his lifestyle, whether he likes the men he is with.

"I don't like any of them."

"They like you."

"Yes ... funny, isn't it? I've often wondered why."[65]

Men with extraordinary looks often cannot recognize or understand the power of their own attraction, and this was the case with Denny. He knew he was beautiful, but as Jim says in the story, anyone could "get a better-looking piece of flesh with a bigger thing for a dollar in any street in this town."[66] Jim's aura of attraction is clearly something more, which mystifies him and fascinates Phillip, what accounts for that instantaneous flash of magic that inexorably draws others to him so that they look at him with thirsty eyes and became fixated on him.

Philip asks Jim about payment for his services. Jim explains that it's not just the money. "I get everything," he said, waving his hand around to encompass the apartment and all that was in it, including the drawings. "One old guy settled a hundred a month on me for life ...Get property ...that's the thing. So many kids, when they start in, just go around chiseling drinks until they get fat and nobody wants them anymore. But I get cash if I can ... or jewelry or pictures. I've learned a lot about painting these last few years. I once spotted a phony Degas some old guy tried to get me to take."[67]

Philip clearly is intrigued.

"You make the deal in advance?" he asked.

"I'm not that crude. I get things without asking. That's what I mean when I say I don't know what it is that they see. I've often thought that if I knew what it was, I'd really be able to cash in."[68]

Philip—here perhaps Vidal himself—gives his theory of the power of Jim's/Denny's appeal: "I suspect," said Philip, "that the fact you don't know may be your charm. Self-consciousness often produced great art but I doubt if many find it a loveable trait, in others. The secret to wide popularity is a kind of mysterious negativity ... something that can't be imitated. Not that I mean you're actually negative, or mysterious (though you may, for all I know, be both), but you give that appearance."[69]

As they talk and drink more Pernod, Jim asks Philip if he likes boys. When Philip answers no, and, upon the next question—"not even once, in school?"—responds no, Jim then inquires "would you like to?" to which Philip responds no, that he's too old to change his habits, and upon further pressing—"you wouldn't like to try?"—declines again the invitation.

They discuss their theories of what men and women are looking for in relationships, and Jim concludes by saying "Damned if I know. I haven't got any theory. All I know is that it's one thing to love somebody and another thing to have sex with somebody you don't know or don't care about, the way I do all the time."[70] Jim continues: "I suppose I've been mauled as much as anybody can be but in spite of all that I think it's possible to care about one person and to forget the acrobatics and think just of him and not the two bodies. But I suppose I'm romantic because I'm just a whore and know how little sex has to do with loving."[71]

The rain has stopped and the two go across the street for dinner.

"They got wonderful snails across the street," Jim said.

"I don't like snails."

"Have you ever tried any?"

"No."

"Well, how do you know?" They both laughed.[72]

After dinner, Jim takes Philip back to his apartment, "just for a moment ... I have to practice my vice."[73]

From a cabinet Jim takes "a yard-long wooden pipe, brightly decorated with Moorish designs," and a thin metal spoon in which he places a single dark pellet and heats it over a Bunsen burner, then pours the heated residue into the pipe, inhaling "so deeply and so long that his face grew red and his eyes stared. Then, slowly, he exhaled a cloud of smoke. Oh, that's good stuff," he said happily, smiling at Philip. That's better than anything I know."[74] He inhales and holds several more times, then hands the pipe to Philip . Like Vidal with Denny, Philip explains to Jim that he doesn't smoke and doesn't know how to inhale.

"Well, it won't work if you can't inhale," agreed Jim. "Anyway you ate the snails. That's enough for one night."

"How do you feel?" asked Philip, curiously.

"Like I'm dreaming ... a little like a dream of flying."

"Better than love?"

"Wouldn't you rather fly than make love?"

"Any day."

"This way I feel like I'm doing both."

"Shall I go?"

"Oh, no ...not yet. Stay with me until I'm way gone. It won't be long."

Jim lays down on the massive bed, patting the edge of the bed for Philip. Like Gore sitting on Denny's bed, Philip sits on Jim's bed as he talks. "But then when he was sure that the other was no longer conscious of him, he got quickly to his feet and, blowing out the paper lantern, he left the apartment."[75]

Jim appears one more time in *The Judgment of Paris*, in a haunting scene written in Joycean stream of consciousness style to recreate Jim's thoughts on an opium trip. Like Denny, Jim has been in a sanitarium and received shock treatments to try to cure him of his addiction, and has been warned by his doctors that his addiction will prove fatal. In this scene, he returns to his apartment after a party, takes out his opium pipe, which is hidden away, finds his last pellet of opium, prepares it, and smokes it. Vidal takes the reader into Jim's dream-like state, learned no doubt through questioning Denny, of drifting, "to the nightmare world of the ceiling across which he must journey, occasionally floating, sometimes running, other times struggling to move even a hand, a finger, as the dreary shadows held him tight above the room, embraced his body with a loving greed, draining it of will and memory ..."[76] Two friends come to visit Jim while he is high and, walking into his apartment and seeing him on the bed, are not sure if he is unconscious or dead. Feeling a pulse, they pull a blanket over him, turn off his Bunsen burner and leave, as he drifts in his haze: "Where was he going? he wondered lazily, as layer after layer of darkness opened to receive him."[77] It is not clear if this is Jim's final trip, but the certainty of death hangs over this scene.

Denny's role in *The Judgment of Paris* is of a minor, secondary character, one of the unusual specimens the narrator meets in his youthful wanderings. It is in one of Vidal's early short stories that a character based on Denham Fouts plays a more pivotal role.

In his memoirs published in 1995, Vidal reveals that he never kept a diary or journal, no record of his days other than "thirteen green pages of notes from 1961 and a diary kept for a month or two in 1948."[78] The notes from 1961 concerned his encounters with President John F. Kennedy in his first year in office, a time when Vidal, who had unsuccessfully run for Congress the year before, still harbored political ambitions; in short, encounters he realized at the time were of special interest and importance. Why would he keep a diary for several months in 1948, the only other time in a very active life during which he kept contemporaneous notes of daily events? Their significance deepens because these were the only pages he would not give to his biographer and are, in fact, the only pages among all of his papers given to the University of Wisconsin, and then transferred to Harvard, to be sealed until "after my death or the Second Coming, whichever comes first."[79] Certainly this year, 1948, was, in Vidal's estimation, an "annus mirabilis" as he called it—a bestseller to his credit, his emergence as a personality, meeting such famed authors as Tennessee Williams, Christopher Isherwood, Paul Bowles, E.M. Forester, Truman Capote—so it would be natural for him to be recording his experiences and thoughts in a journal. But these are not the sorts of jottings to be kept secret.

Clues to this mystery may well be found in a short story Vidal wrote in 1956 in that octagonal library at Edgewater with its views of the gardens and the Hudson and the Catskills. "Pages From an Abandoned Journal" (certainly the title of the story is intriguing: pages from a diary begun in 1948 and put aside after two months) was published in a collection of his short stories written between 1948 and 1956, titled *A Thirsty Evil*.

The story opens with the narrator's journal entry for April 30, 1948. (It would be interesting if Vidal's diary fragment from 1948 started on that exact date, which was, in fact, five days after Vidal met Christopher Isherwood, and three days after he first met Denham Fouts.) Peter, an American from Toledo, Ohio (representative, perhaps, of the norm, of middle America) in Paris working on his doctorate on Nero and the Civil Wars, has been at a bar the night before where he "told everyone off" and apparently rebuffed the advances of Steven, another patron at the bar. "I said I wasn't interested, that I didn't mind what other people did, etc., just as long as they left me alone, that I was getting married in the fall when I got back to the states (WRITE HELEN) and that I don't go in for any of that, never did and never will. I also told him in no uncertain terms that it's very embarrassing for a grown man to be treated like some idiot girl surrounded by a bunch of seedy, middle-aged Don Juans trying to get their hooks into her ...him."[80]

To Peter's surprise, Steven calls the next morning and invites him to a party at Elliott Magren's apartment. Elliott Magren is the Denham Fouts character in this short story, and, appropriately enough, lives on the Rue du Bac, just as Denny did. Peter is curious about Elliott, who is "already a legend in Europe,"[81] and so decides to go to the party.

When Peter arrives at the apartment at ten-thirty that night, Steven greets him at the door—"The beautiful Peter!"— and shows him through the four large rooms of the apartment to the last room, where Elliott, dressed, lays on a big bed surrounded by pillows. The room is dimly lit by lamps with red shades, and over the bed hangs a painting of a nude man, "the work of a famous painter I'd never heard of."[82] In the room with Steven and Peter are a dozen other men, middle-aged, in expensive suits. Steven introduces Peter to Elliott, who shakes his hand and pulls him next to him on the bed, and asks if he wants to smoke opium. Peter told him no, he doesn't use drugs.

Peter doesn't find this legend to be unusually handsome, certainly not movie star glamorous as he had expected. "He is about five foot ten and weighs about a hundred sixty pounds. He has dark, straight hair that falls over his forehead; his eyes were black. The two sides of his face don't match, like Oscar Wilde's. Because of drugs, he is unnaturally pale."[83] That description matches Vidal's description in his memoirs of his first meeting with Denny. In fact, Vidal's depiction of Elliott in this short story so closely matches Denham Fouts that it seems a fair assumption that the story follows closely what Denny told the author about the start of his career.

In "Pages from an Abandoned Journal," Elliott grew up in Galveston, Texas and at sixteen was befriended by a German baron who spotted him on the beach and took him to Berlin. In a parenthetical remark in the short story, Peter raises the sort of question that surrounds Denny's life story: "I always wonder about details in a story like this: what did his parents say about a stranger walking off with their son? Was there a scene? Did they know what was going on?"[84] Elliott spends several years with the baron, then has a fight and begins walking from Berlin to Munich when a limousine pulls over and an old Egyptian shipping magnate in the back seat invites Elliott into the car and ends up taking him on his yacht for a cruise of the Mediterranean. In Naples, Elliott and a Greek sailor on the yacht steal several thousand dollars from the old man, jump ship, and make their way to Capri where they stay at the most expensive hotel. In the short story, the sailor leaves, Elliott can't pay his bills and is about to be led off to jail "when Lord Glenellen, who was just checking into the hotel, saw him and told the police to let him go, that *he* would pay his bill ..."[85]

Lord Glenellen takes Elliott to England, just as Evan Morgan, Lord Tredegar, saved Denny from arrest in Capri and took him on a world tour and then home to Tredegar House. In the short story, Elliott, moving in higher aristocratic circles, meets Prince Basil and lives with him until he becomes King Basil. In Denny's life, it was Prince Paul who became King Paul. When war threatens Europe, Elliott goes to California where he tries to "get interested in Vedanta and tries to stop taking drugs and lead a quiet ... if not normal ... life," just as Denny went to California, stayed with Christopher Isherwood, studied Vedanta, and entered college.[86] After the War, Elliott returns to Paris and the Rue du Bac, as did Denny.

As they sit together on the bed, Steven brings Elliott his opium pipe. Elliott lights up and begins to talk. "I can't remember a word he said. I was aware, though, that this was probably the most brilliant conversation I'd ever heard. It might have been the setting which was certainly provocative or maybe I'd inhaled some of the opium which put me in a receptive mood but, no matter the cause, I sat listening to him, fascinated, not wanting him to stop."[87] So Gore sat on Denny's bed, listening, absorbing.

With his eyes shut (the opium made them sensitive to the light), Elliott asks Peter about himself. Peter tells him about growing up in Toledo, Ohio, his work at Columbia for his doctorate, his plans to marry Helen and teach—in short, his plans for a normal, all-American life—"but as I talked I couldn't help but think how dull my life must sound to Elliott. I cut it short. I couldn't compete with him," and then Peter adds, "and didn't want to."[88] Here is a first subtle sign that Peter finds his new acquaintance of special interest.

In his entry of May 25, 1948, Peter is at the beach at Deauville with Hilda, a high school friend from Toledo who he met in Paris and with whom he has begun an affair, although "having sex with her is about the dullest pastime I can think of."[89] Elliott appears, walking down the beach in crimson swim trunks and sunglasses, and Peter notices "with surprise how smooth and youthful his body was, like a boy."[90] Is Elliott there by chance, or by design? That night they had first met in Elliott's bedroom, Elliott had asked Peter "if I'd see him some evening alone, and I said I would like to but ...and this was completely spur of the moment ...I said I was going to Deauville the next day, with a girl."[91] Is Peter afraid of being alone with Elliott? Does he want to confirm to Elliott, and to himself, that he is straight? Has Elliott followed Peter there?

Two days later, Peter and Hilda see Elliott again at the hotel where they are staying, though now in tow was a fourteen-year-old boy Elliott introduces to them. The next morning, after Hilda leaves for Paris, Peter knocks on Elliott's door, as Elliott has asked him to do, to meet him and go with him to the beach. In the room, Elliott and the fourteen year old are sitting on the floor, naked, working on assembling a Meccano erector set, the blueprints and parts spread about them. "The boy who was the color of a terra-cotta pot gave me a wicked grin."[92] From this description, it seems that Vidal had met Gerard at Denny's apartment, or at least had heard all about him—the teenager Denny had met on a beach in Brittany, taken by his resemblance to himself. That "wicked grin" mirrors Michael Wishart's description of Gerard's "wide, violet, conqueror's eyes." Vidal had realized right away when he met Denny that Denny "was at his best with pubescent boys."[93]

Elliott and the teenager put on swim trunks and, together, the three walk to the beach where the teenager goes off on his own. "I asked Elliott if this sort of thing wasn't very dangerous and he said yes it probably was but life was short and he was afraid of nothing, except drugs. He told me then that he had had an electrical shock treatment at a clinic shortly before I'd first met him. Now, at last, he was off opium and he hoped it was a permanent cure ... Then when I asked him if he always went in for young boys he said yes and made a joke about how, having lost all memory of his own childhood, he would have to live out a new one with some boy."[94]

A pivotal point in the short story, and perhaps in Vidal's life, is revealed in the entry from the abandoned journal for May 29, 1948. It is evening; Andre, the fourteen-year-old boy, has gone home to his family. Peter and Elliott are having dinner together on the hotel's terrace overlooking the sea. (In an oral history, Vidal spoke of dining with Denny a number of times after their first meeting in Denny's bedroom.) The two characters in the story begin to reveal more about themselves to each other:

> Eating fresh sole from the Channel, I told Elliott all about Jimmie, told him things I myself had nearly forgotten, had wanted to forget. I told him how it had started at twelve and gone on, without plan or thought or even acknowledgement until, at seventeen, I went to the Army and he to the Marines and a quick death. After the Army, I met Helen and forgot him completely; his death, like Elliott's shock treatment, took with it all memory, a thousand summer days abandoned on a coral island.[95]

Here again, in a style reminiscent of Hemingway's reliance on what is left out of a story, what is not told, to give it emotional depth, is the Jimmie Trimble story. Gore already had told Tennessee Williams all about Jimmie, and Christopher Isherwood's diaries from these days reveal that Vidal had told him of his love for Jimmie.[96] That he would share this story with Denny when they were together hints at the intimacies of their conversation.

Finishing his story, Peter wonders why he had told Elliott, feeling as if he had said too much: why was he telling his new acquaintance that which revealed the innermost secrets he had not accepted himself? Elliott contemplated silently what he had heard, then spoke to Peter "about life and duty to oneself and how the moment is all one has and how it is dishonorable to cheat oneself of that." Peter thinks about this "strange disjointed speech." As he writes in his journal: "I'm not sure that he said anything very useful or very original but sitting there in the dark, listening, his words had a peculiar urgency for me and I felt, in a way, that I was listening to an oracle . . ."[97]

Could this be the turning point when Peter/Gore came to grips with their own identity, their own sexuality, who they were? Could Denny have had this sort of impact on Gore's life?

In the short story's journal entry three days later, June 1, 1948, we learn that Elliott has been arrested. Young Andre has stolen his camera; Andre's parents find the camera and ask where he got it; under threats from them, Andre tells his parents that Elliott has tried to seduce him. A gendarme comes to Peter while he was sitting on the hotel's terrace and tells him that Elliott Magren has asked him to visit him in jail, and then questions him about what he knows about Mr. Magren, looking at him suspiciously. "It was only too apparent what his opinion of *me* was: another *pederast americain*. My voice shook and my throat dried up as I told him I hardly knew Elliott ... I'd only just met him ... I knew nothing about his private life."[98] In his journal entry for this day, Peter records the events as if from a distance. "All I wanted was to get away

116

from Deauville, from Elliott, from the crime ... and it *was* a crime, I'm sure of that."[99] Frightened, Peter immediately packs his bags and that day returns to Paris. "I'm not proud of my cowardice but I didn't want to be drawn into something I hardly understood."[100] Several days later, he records in his diary that Steven told him how Elliott had contacted a friend who was a lawyer, the charges were dropped, perhaps through a payment, and Elliott is staying in Deauville for another week "doubtless to be near Andre."[101]

The journal's next entry is dated December 26, 1953: almost six years have elapsed. Peter is now in New York City, hung-over from a Christmas party where an English playwright he met had "made the biggest play for me," though, Peter notes, he wasn't at all attractive.[102] Peter is now an antiques dealer; he has sold to Steven a Queen Anne desk for his new apartment where Peter went with Steven after the party. There, Steven questions Peter about Bob and his break-up with Bob. At first it seems as if this concerns the break-up of a business arrangement, but the context makes it clear that it is also the break-up of a personal relationship. "Well, I'm out of it and any day now I'll meet somebody ...though it's funny how seldom you see anyone who's really attractive. There was a nice young Swede at Steven's but I never did get his name and anyway he is being kept by that ribbon clerk from the Madison Avenue Store."[103] Clearly, Peter in the intervening years has come out.

The next day, the narrator goes to a tea at the home of Mrs. Blaine-Smith, an important patron to whom he has sold a Hepplewhite sofa and a lot of other antiques. Another guest at the tea party is an Italian count "who was terribly nice though unattractive"[104]; the two exchange stories about their times in Europe after World War II. "Then, as always, the name Elliott Magren was mentioned. He's practically a codeword ... if you know Elliott, well, you're on the inside and of course the Count (as I'd expected all along) knew Elliott and we exchanged bits of information about him, skirting carefully drugs and small boys." The two talk about Elliott's apartment "and that marvelous Tchelichew [note how Peter now knows the artist's name] that hangs over his bed" when another of the guests, an Englishman, tells them that Elliott Magren has died the week before. The Count is visibly upset, and Peter wonders if he had been one of Elliott's lovers.

And then a stunner: Peter writes in his journal: "I couldn't help recalling then that terrible time at Deauville when Elliott was arrested and I had to put up bail for him and hire a lawyer, all in French!"[105] "I"? This Peter had not been able to admit, even in his journal, as those events unfolded almost six years before: that it was he who thought enough of Elliott, who was close enough to Elliott, to come to his rescue.

The news of Elliott's death brings back to Peter memories of those months in 1948: "what an important summer that was, the chrysalis burst at last. . ."[106]

In itself, "Pages from an Abandoned Journal" would not be a memorable short story, certainly not one that would have found its way into an anthology of the best short stories of the decade, or even one that would be remembered long after it is read. Nevertheless, its an intriguing story that may be read on a number of levels. It is a subtly unfolding, finely wrought coming-of-age story of Peter's awakening to his sexuality, his identity, with Elliott perhaps as a catalyst who opened his eyes—the oracle—to the importance of being true to oneself, of the importance of the moment. This story adheres so closely to the details of Denny's life that it perhaps is not a reckless leap to conclude that it is a close transcription of the secret pages from Vidal's journal locked away with his papers at Harvard. In all of his voluminous and often introspective writings, Vidal never analyzes his transformation from the man at the Christmas party at Mrs. Shippen's Dancing School that December in 1942, telling Jimmie Trimble of his plans to marry Rosalind while "coming simultaneously" with Jimmie in the basement men's room stall, to the man who lived with Howard Austen from 1952 until his partner's death in 2003. Did Vidal's encounters with Denham Fouts hold the key to his own awakening, the time when his own "chrysalis burst"? Certainly the year 1948, the year he repeatedly called that "annus mirabilis," a time when "those of us who had missed our youth tried to catch up,"[107] had a special meaning in his life. If so, this quiet short story may someday be viewed as a key to Gore Vidal's life story, and as a nonfiction chronicle of Denham Fouts.

CHAPTER SEVEN

"DENNY HAD REAL MAGIC"

That photograph! That photograph of twenty-four-year-old Truman Capote that appeared on the dust jacket of his first novel, *Other Voices, Other Rooms*, published in January of 1948, a few days after the publication of Gore Vidal's *The City and the Pillar*; that photograph which Denny had seen in *Life* magazine and cut out and kept next to his bed under his opium pipe; that photograph that showed the young author reclining on a Victorian sofa, looking ten years younger than his actual age, drilling the camera with smoldering eyes, his right hand touching himself suggestively; that photograph that Capote had carefully staged, which became perhaps the most famous, infamous, photograph ever to grace a book jacket and drew endless attention to the novel and its ambitious author: that photograph had captured the imagination of Denham Fouts.

Word of the new literary sensation already had spread to London and Paris even before *Other Voices, Other Rooms* was published anywhere in Europe. "Truman Capote is all the rage here," Peter Watson's lover, Waldemar Hansen, wrote from London on May 6, 1948 to a friend in the United States, noting he had heard that Denny had sent the beguiling young author a blank check with but one word written on it: "Come." "So now," Hansen added, "Capote will be turning up in Paris soon."[1]

120

Waldemar, who had met Truman in New York City, knew his friend well. Capote set sail on the *Queen Elizabeth* on May 14, joining the throng of Americans flocking to Europe after the War. Waldemar met him in London and introduced him to the luminaries he had come to know through Peter Watson. "Truman wasn't interested in seeing things like the Tower of London," Waldemar remembered; rather, he wanted to meet everyone who was anybody, and, together, they made the rounds, visiting Cecil Beaton, Somerset Maugham, Evelyn Waugh, Nöel Coward. In return, Truman reveled in his role as confidante to Waldemar, advising him on how to save his deteriorating relationship with Peter Watson. "If you're going to be a grand courtesan," Truman instructed, "you've got to play hard to get. Let's beard the lion in his den!"[2]

The two set off for Paris where Peter, to distance himself from Denny, was staying at the Pont Royal Hotel on the Rue du Bac. Waldemar followed Truman's advice and told Peter he hadn't come to Paris to see him, but rather to show his American friend around the city. It worked. Truman orchestrated a reconciliation between the two, and Waldemar credited Truman's counsel with restoring his relationship with Peter.

Waldemar had warned Truman about Denny, about how much of a burden he could become. "Even when he was perfectly well," Christopher Isherwood's friend—Bill Harris recalled from their Santa Monica days, "Denny would often be propped up in bed, like a little boy who's sick and waiting for friends to come and visit him. He wanted to be taken care of forever."[3] Keep your distance, Waldemar had cautioned his visitor, words that of course made Truman all the more eager to make the pilgrimage to 44 Rue du Bac.

The two Southerners hit it off instantly. Both liked to exaggerate their deep South accents (Capote said Denny talked "as though his mouth were busy with a pound of

Alabama corn mush"),[4] both were a curious mixture of innocence and experience, both were more than happy to have others dote on them. Decades later Capote was asked in an interview what he would have been if he hadn't become a writer. An attorney, he answered, and then added, "also, I wouldn't have minded being kept, but no one has ever wanted to keep me—not more than a week or so."[5] Truman was fascinated to be with the world's most famous kept man, while Denny was fascinated to be with an author who had achieved the exact sort of lionization he dreamed about when he had started writing a novel while living with Christopher Isherwood. And that photograph on the jacket of *Other Voices, Other Rooms* had not been misleading. Isherwood described Truman as looking like "a sort of cuddly little Koala bear."[6] The author could easily pass for a teenager—blue puppy dog eyes, silken blond bangs, pouty-lipped, an instantly infectious smile and laugh, a natural ebullience: at last Denny had found his own fantasy. As Gore Vidal had remarked, Denny "was at his best with pubescent boys; but then he was one himself, I should think, a southern Penrod who still spoke with a North Florida accent."[7] Truman looked the part to perfection.

Truman found that Denny "was more conversationalist than sensualist; ...though he wanted us to share the same bed, his interest in me was romantic but not sexual."[8] Denny's libido had been damaged by his addiction, but he was content just to have Truman worship him as he entranced Truman.

Truman spent hours lying with Denny on the massive bed beneath Tchelitchev's *Adonis*, gossiping and listening to his stories. Like everyone else, Truman was smitten: "Denny radiated a quality that was the exact opposite of what he was, extraordinary health, youth, and unspoiled innocence. Whatever he had done the night before, or the day before, or the week before, he always looked as if he had just awakened on the freshest and most beautiful morning in the world. To watch him walk into a room was an experience. He was beyond being good-looking: he was the single most charming-looking person I've ever seen."[9]

Those first days of June, Truman stayed with Denny in the "high-ceilinged dusk of those shuttered, meandering rooms."[10] Often in the afternoon, they would go to Champs-Elysées movies, "and at some juncture [Denny] always, having begun slightly to sweat, hurried to the men's room and dosed himself with drugs; in the evening he inhaled opium or sipped opium tea, a concoction he brewed by boiling in water the crust of opium that had accumulated inside his pipe. But he was not a nodder; I never saw him drug-dazed or enfeebled."[11] The two became friends. "Denny had real magic and I adored him. But I was frightened of him and the drug scene. I was young, and I didn't plan to get involved in any of that. I wanted to get him off drugs, and he also wanted to get out of the life he had been living all those years. He loved the West and he had a fantasy about buying a gasoline station in Arizona, the sort of place that has a sign saying, 'Last Chance for Gas for Fifty Miles.' I was going to write, and he was going to run it and be cured of all the things that were wrong with him."[12] This fantasy they spun together was a variation of one of the plans Peter and Denny had contemplated before the War, of moving to Arizona and growing oranges.

Truman had enough influence over Denny to persuade him to enter a Swiss drug rehabilitation clinic; as always, whenever Denny found a new friend, his interest in living revived. The two "said good-bye at the Gare de Lyon; he was somewhat high on something and looked, with his fresh-colored face—the face of a severe, avengeful angel—twenty years old. His rattling conversation ranged from filling stations to the fact that he had once visited Tibet. At last Denny said, "if it goes wrong, please do this: destroy everything that's mine. Burn all my clothes. My letters. I wouldn't want Peter having the pleasure.'"[13] They agreed that when Denny's treatment was complete, they would meet in Italy to celebrate.

But Truman had no intention of meeting Denny there, or anywhere. As with Christopher Isherwood, Gore Vidal, and all his visitors, Denny had handed his opium pipe to Capote: "Denny offered me drugs, but I refused, and he never insisted, though once he said: 'Scared?' Yes, but not of drugs; it was Denny's derelict life that frightened me, and I wanted to emulate him not at all."[14] Capote had caught a glimpse of what his own future might hold—Denny as the ghost of Christmas Future—and its reality horrified him.

As usual, Denny's commitment to change his habits didn't last long. By mid-June, Truman was writing to Waldemar: "Our disturbing friend just called. The Switzerland deal seems to be off. It makes me feel like a miserable heel, but what can I do now but wash my hands of the whole affair?"[15] Just as Waldemar had warned him, he came to see that "Denny was ...an ominous presence, a heavy passenger— I felt if I didn't free myself that, like Sinbad and the burdensome Old Man, I'd have to cart Denny piggyback the rest of his life."[16]

Capote's feelings of guilt over deserting Denny surfaced decades later in his novel *Answered Prayers*; there he recounts the heartbreaking story of Bob, a sixty-year-old blind man staying at the Y.M.C.A. in Manhattan; ten years before, he had married Helen, a waitress. Now, when he was in the hospital for an operation on his leg, she comes to tell him she is leaving him, taking their truck, taking their aluminum trailer home, and leaving him with nothing but a suitcase with his clothes. When he gets out of the hospital, he hitch-hikes from California to New York City. Capote compared this story to his desertion of Denny in the clinic: "A helpless man waiting in the dark by the side of an unknown road; that's how Denny Fouts must have felt, for I had been as heartless to him as Helen had been to Bob."[17]

Truman left Paris and on July 4 arrived in Venice, his repertoire now enhanced as he spoke of his "dear acquaintance" Denny Fouts, the legend already growing so that Denny had "slept with just everyone—Jean Marais, King Farouk, the Maharaja so-and-so . . ."[18] Denny's story kept percolating in his thoughts, assuming a central role in his ideas about a book he had begun to believe would be his magnum opus; but it would be years before his new friend's strange story would find its way into his fiction.

Capote's reputation always far exceeded his slim output. *A Tree of Night*, a collection of eight short stories, was published in January of 1949, followed by *Local Color* in 1950, and *The Grass Harp*, a novel based on his Alabama childhood, in 1951. *The Muses Are Heard*, an account of his travels through the Soviet Union with the cast of *Porgy and Bess*, appeared in 1956, and his short masterpiece, *Breakfast at Tiffany's*, in 1958. It was during these years, as he wrote these gem-like stories, that he was adopted by high society as a sort of mascot. Woman of wealth and stature found him amusing, witty, charming, the most delightful company; and where they led, their powerful husbands followed. It wasn't long before Truman was on a first name basis with those who graced the highest reaches of New York and international society—Babe Paley, Lee Radziwill, Gloria Vanderbilt, Slim Keith, C.Z. Guest, Gloria Guinness, Marella Agnelli—a fixture at their dinners and parties, a guest at their country homes and Caribbean retreats. As it turned out, as he was singing for his supper, entertaining his society friends, he was mining material for his magnum opus.

After completing his work on *Breakfast at Tiffany's* in 1957, Capote began to focus more on this work that had always been in his thoughts, making notes and outlines and preliminary sketches, drawing material from the stories he had heard gossiping with his new friends. He already had the title, *Answered Prayers*, taken from a saying of St. Theresa that "more tears are shed over answered prayers than unanswered ones."[19] On September 29, 1958, while staying at Paros on

Greece, Truman wrote to Bennett Cerf at Random House, reporting that he was working on "a large novel, my magnum opus, a book about which I must be very silent so as not to alarm my 'sitters' and which I think will really arouse you when I outline it (only you must never mention it to a soul). The novel is called *Answered Prayers*; and if all goes well, I think it will answer mine."[20] His mention of his "sitters" was a reference to his society friends, an early recognition that they might be offended by the subject of this book.

Answered Prayers had always seemed the book Capote was destined to write. Christopher Isherwood remembered the first time he met Truman. It was May 1, 1947: Christopher was having lunch with Bennett Cerf, also his editor at Random House. Capote's first novel, *Other Voices, Other Rooms*, was still months from publication, but the editor that day taking Truman around the offices assured Isherwood 'that this young man could only be compared to Proust.' And then the marvelously gracious little baby personage itself appeared; Truman sailed into the room with his right hand extended, palm downward, as if he expected [me] to kiss it. [I] didn't, but within a few moments [I] was quite ready to—having been almost instantaneously conquered by the campy Capote charm. To hell with Proust; here was something infinitely rarer and more amusing, a live Ronald Firbank character!"[21] The two became friends, and always Isherwood was urging Capote to write the book he was sure was in him. "Somehow or other (and I've said this to him constantly), I feel that he hasn't yet quite written about the things that he'd be best at writing about. I always say to him, 'why don't you be our New York Proust? Why don't you write about feuds and social goings-on in Manhattan?' because he knows this stuff inside out ... I'm sure that he could do wonderful things on the largest scale showing the whole nature of society today."[22] Norman Mailer, too, who had called Capote "the most perfect writer of my generation,"[23] was convinced of it: "I would suspect," Mailer commented in 1959, "he hesitates between the attractions of Society, which enjoys and so repays him for his unique gifts, and the novel he could write of the gossip column's real life, a major work, but it would banish him forever from his favorite world. Since I have nothing to lose, I hope Truman fries a few of the fancier fish."[24] Capote was sure of it himself: "I am not Proust. I am not as intelligent or as educated as he was. I am not as sensitive in various ways. But my eye is every bit as good as his. Every bit! I see everything! I don't miss nothin'! If Proust were an American living now in New York, this is what he would be doing."[25]

Capote never would forget the day he put on hold the Proustian masterpiece he and Isherwood and Mailer knew was his. It was a Monday, November 16, 1959, and there, deep inside the *New York Times*, page thirty-nine, was a headline "WEALTHY FARMER, 3 of Family Slain" and a one column story that caught his attention, a bare bones account of a murder in Holcomb, Kansas the day before: "A wealthy wheat farmer, his wife and their two young children were found shot to death today in their home. They had been killed by shotgun blasts at close range after being bound and gagged."[26]

He read it and read it again, and again. At the time, he had been toying with the notion that "journalism, reportage, could be forced to yield a serious new art form: the 'nonfiction novel' as I thought of it."[27] It wasn't that this crime itself was of special interest to him. Rather, the crime, this story, could provide the framework for his literary experiment, "a book that would read exactly like a novel except that every word of it would be absolutely true."[28] He thought about it. "Everything would seem freshly minted. The people, their accents and attitude, the landscape, its contours, the weather. All this, it seemed to me, could only sharpen my eye and quicken my ear." The more he thought about it, the more it felt right. "Well, why not *this* crime? The Clutter case. Why not pack up and go to Kansas and see what happens?"[29]

By mid-December, he was on his way, accompanied by his childhood friend from Alabama, Nelle Harper Lee, who had just completed her novel *To Kill a Mockingbird* and, awaiting publication date, was ready for adventure.

When the elfin Capote with the voice of a fourth grader arrived deep in the heart of middle America, dressed in a large sheepskin coat, a pillbox hat, a long scarf wrapped around his neck with the ends dragging down to his moccasins, the citizens of Holcomb were stunned. It was Nelle Harper Lee who saved the day. "Nelle walked into the kitchen," one resident of the town remembered, "and five minutes later I felt I had known her for a long time."[30] By the time the two left Kansas in the middle of January 1960, they were treated as celebrities. Within the month, Capote had signed a book contract with Random House and by April had started writing the book he would call *In Cold Blood*.

He estimated that it would take about a year to complete and went to Verbier, Switzerland where he bought a small condominium to avoid all the distractions of the social life he loved in New York City. "Gregariousness is the enemy of art, so when I work, I have to forcibly remove myself from other people. I'm like a prizefighter in training: I have to sweep all the elements except work out of my life completely."[31] On June 27, 1960, he would write to Bennett Cerf: "I'm all right. Living quietly; see literally no one; and am totally concentrated on *IN COLD BLOOD*. My enthusiasm is as high as ever. No, higher. It is going to be a masterpiece."[32]

But it wasn't long before this first burst of enthusiasm began to wane and strains began to appear. He called Verbier a "very pretty, very remote, very healthy, extremely snowbound, and unalterably boring village."[33] By September, he was writing to a friend "what an appalling and terrible story it is. This is the last time I am ever going to write 'a reportage.'"[34] He found that being alone for so long a period was "rather frightening. Something about it was unsettling,"[35] and working with that subject matter "led to a definite darkness and terrific apprehension. I've never been so nervous and so agitated. I never slept more than three hours a night."[36] He would admit that "this sort of sustained creative work keeps one in a constant state of tension, and when one adds to it all these other uncertainties and anxieties, the strain is just too much. I'll tell you something: every morning of my life I throw up because of the tensions created by the writing of this book. But it's worth it; because it's the best work I've done."[37]

The work, the tension, the concerns of whether putting so much time into one book would pay off, the trips back to Kansas for more research, and back to the isolation and loneliness of secluding himself to write dragged on. In August of 1961 he had estimated he had at least another year's work on the book; "with great industry, and nothing but solid luck, I might be able to finish in a year this September."[38] But six months later, on February 25, 1962, he would write to Cecil Beaton, who had been a friend since Waldemar Hansen introduced them in London in 1948: "I figure I have another 18 months to go, by which time I should be good and nuts."[39] It was not until three years later that he would write to Beaton that "I'm finishing the last pages of my book—I must be rid of it regardless of what happens. I hardly give a fuck anymore what happens. My sanity is at stake—and that is no mere idle phrase. Oh the hell with it."[40] Six months after that he again wrote to him, "Finished the final pages of my book three days ago. Bless Jesus. But incredible to suddenly be free (comparatively) of all those years and years of tension and aging. At the moment, only feel bereft. But grateful. Never again!"[41]

In Cold Blood did indeed answer the author's prayers, and in spades. Even before the book was complete, even before it was excerpted in *The New Yorker*, he was being offered substantial sums for the movie rights—$250,000 from Twentieth Century-Fox, $300,000 from Frank Sinatra, eventually landing through his agent a million dollar contract, later selling the paperback rights for $500,000, and the foreign and book club publication rights for another million dollars—all before publication. When at last the book was published in January of 1966, it rode the bestseller lists for months, earning him millions more. Even more important to him, he had become the most recognized living American author.

And for a while, he basked in the glory.

All summer he sat by the pool of a Bridgehampton friend, writing in a school composition notebook, not sketching the outline of his next book, *Answered Prayers*, but rather preparing a list of names, adding to it and deleting from it, joking with whoever learned what he was doing: "well, maybe you'll be invited and maybe you won't,"[42] refining his list to the select five hundred who would receive invitations to what he already was calling "the party of the century."

It would be held in the ballroom of Manhattan's Plaza Hotel on a Monday night, November 28, 1966: a Black and White Ball. The dress code was set forth very specifically on the handwritten invitations sent out in October:

Gentlemen: Black Tie; Black Mask
Ladies: Black or White Dress;
White Mask; Fan

He chose as the guest of honor Katherine Graham, owner of the *Washington Post*, but there was no doubt that this party was his, his reward for his years of toil on *In Cold Blood*, a celebration of its overwhelming success, and certainly the fulfillment of a fantasy. "Don't you think Truman sat there in Monroeville, Alabama, when he was about ten" his friend, John Knowles, author of *A Separate Peace*, mused, "deeply rejected and out of it, strange little outcast, even in his own house, and said that someday he would hire the most beautiful ballroom in New York City and he would have the most elegant and famous people in the world there?"[43]

130

The invitation list represented a startling intersection of the social, political, and literary worlds: Frank Sinatra and Mia Farrow, Babe and William Paley, Gloria Guinness, Marella Agnelli, Cecil Beaton, Lillian Hellman, Mr. and Mrs. Henry Ford, Harper Lee, Tallulah Bankhead, Norman Mailer, William F. Buckley, Jr., Lee Radziwell, Christopher Isherwood, Capote's friends from Kansas who were the cast of *In Cold Blood*, Alice Roosevelt Longworth, Candice Bergen, the doorman from the U.N. Plaza apartments where he lived, Leonard Bernstein, Noël Coward, Walter Cronkite, David Merrick, Sammy Davis and Tennessee Williams, among others. "It was one of those rare occasions," John Kenneth Galbraith remembered, "when you knew by sight or by fame or infamy everybody there."[44]

But after a while, after the distraction of the party, he felt completely drained by the effort *In Cold Blood* had consumed. "I certainly wouldn't do it again. If I knew or had known when I started it what was going to be involved, I never would have started it, regardless of what the result would have been."[45] He said later that if he had realized what lay ahead of him as he and Harper Lee drove toward Kansas "I would have driven straight on. Like a bat out of hell."[46]

A bitterness crept into his thoughts as he began to feel that others had imitated his groundbreaking idea of the nonfiction novel, including Norman Mailer's *The Armies of the Night*, Woodward and Bernstein's *All the President's Men*: "They got all the prizes and I got nothing. And I felt I deserved them. The decisions not to give them to me were truly, totally unjust. So at that point I said 'Fuck you! All of you! If you are so unjust and don't know when something is unique and original and great, then fuck you! I don't care about you anymore, or want to have anything to do with you. If you can't appreciate something really extraordinary like *In Cold Blood* and the five-and-a-half years I put into it, and all of the artistry and the style and the skill, then fuck you'!"[47]

Capote could sense himself how he had changed. "No one will ever know what *In Cold Blood* took out of me. It scraped me right down to the marrow of my bones. It nearly killed me. I think, in a way, it *did* kill me. Before I began it, I was a stable person, comparatively speaking. Afterward, something happened to me."[48] John Knowles, too, felt something fundamental had happened to his friend and also traced the roots of Capote's depression to *In Cold Blood*: "It was such an overwhelming success in every way, critically, financially. I think he lost a grip on himself after that. He had been tremendously disciplined up to that time. One of the most disciplined writers I've ever met. But he couldn't sustain it after that. A lot of his motivation was lost. That's when he began to unravel."[49]

Even while writing his non-fiction novel, Capote had been thinking about *Answered Prayers,* which he had begun in 1958. On August 22, 1964, he had written to Bennett Cerf: "*In Cold Blood*' is nearly completed; I'm taking a few weeks away from it to write an outline of the novel I intend to write this winter. I will let you read the outline."[50] But with the final push to complete *In Cold Blood*, and then the frenzy surrounding its publication, it was not until January 5, 1966 that he signed a contract with Random House for this next book and received on signing, an advance against future royalties of $25,000. This contract, which he felt confident enough to negotiate himself, called for a manuscript delivery date of January 1, 1968—two years to write a relatively short novel that had to be no more than a guaranteed minimum of two hundred and fifty pages.

Neither the manuscript nor any sentence of it was delivered on January 1, 1968, and in May of 1969 the contract was re-worked as a three book contract with the delivery date of *Answered Prayers* moved ahead to January 1973, and the advance increased based on the success of *In Cold Blood*. In 1967, Twentieth Century-Fox had bought, for $350,000, the movie rights to *Answered Prayers*, a huge sum for a book whose first sentence Capote has not yet shown to anyone. When the manuscript of the book had not been delivered by the contractual deadline, Capote had to pay back to Fox $200,000, the first installment payment he had received for the movie rights. The pressure to produce was tightening on him. " ...I have a novel," he had written to a friend, "something on a large and serious scale, that pursues me like a crazy wind."[51] Early in 1973 the delivery date was pushed to January 1974, and six months later changed to September 1977. Then in 1980, fourteen years after the original contract was signed, the completion date was changed again, now to March 1, 1981, and the advance raised to $1,000,000 on delivery of the manuscript.

What had happened?

Always a slow writer, his output became glacial as he enjoyed the life of a celebrity and as he began to drink more heavily and to abuse prescription drugs, admitting also that he was using cocaine every day at a cost of about $60,000 a year.[52]

As the years slipped by with nothing to show, he began justifying his time saying that he had spent four years, from 1968 through 1972, "reading and selecting, rewriting and indexing my own letters, other people's letters, my diaries and journals (which contained detailed accounts of hundreds of scenes and conversations) for the years 1943 through 1965"[53] for use in *Answered Prayers*. In 1972, he finally began writing, working on the last chapter of the book first, then the first chapter "Unspoiled Monsters," then the fifth which he called "A Severe Insult to the Brain," and then the seventh, "La Côte Basque."

The alcohol, the drugs, the temptations of celebrity may have robbed him of the discipline he had mustered while writing *In Cold Blood*, but the real blow to his work-in-progress came in 1975 when he made the decision, against his publisher's recommendation, to begin publishing a few chapters of his novel-in-progress in *Esquire*.

The first chapter he selected for publication in the December 1975 issue was to be a middle chapter of the novel. "La Cote Basque" included not only characters clearly identifiable as his society friends, but also some characters with the same names as these friends, and featured a rich stew of scandalous tidbits they had told him in confidence.

Capote had been quite sure his friends would view *Answered Prayers* as a work of art and not be troubled by their appearances in it, and, in fact, be delighted to be a part of a work by such a famous author. He was blind-sided by their instant cries of outrage and betrayal. At once, they cut him from their lives. He was expelled from Olympus. "I can't understand why everybody's so upset," he said. "What did they think they had around them, a court jester? They had a writer."[54]

Capote put on a brave front and when another chapter, "Unspoiled Monsters," was published in *Esquire* in May 1976, he poked fun at the outcry, appearing on the magazine's cover dressed in black as an assassin fondling a stiletto. "Capote Strikes Again" the cover read; "More from *Answered Prayers*: The Most Talked About Book of the Year."[55]

"Unspoiled Monsters," the second chapter Capote wrote for *Answered Prayers*, was intended to be the opening chapter of the novel, a key to the entire book. It's strange title came from an eight year old's rumination he had happened upon: "If I could do anything, I would go to the middle of our planet, Earth, and seek uranium, rubies, and gold. I'd look for Unspoiled Monsters."

The narrator of this section is P.B. Jones. Jones, who has been described as a male Holly Golightly from *Breakfast at Tiffany's*, is also an alter ego of the author, perhaps his imaginings of the course of his life had his early short stories not been accepted for publication and his career as an author had not fallen so neatly into place. Jones is in his mid-thirties and has had the same sort of fantastical early years as Capote long ago had invented for himself for his author's write-up on the book jacket of *Other Voices, Other Rooms*: "written speeches for a third-rate politician, danced on a river boat, made a small fortune painting flowers on glass, read scripts for a film company, studied fortune telling with the celebrated Mrs. Acey Jones, worked on *The New Yorker*, and selected anecdotes for a digest magazine. . ."[56] As Capote explained: "P.B. isn't me, but on the other hand he isn't not me. His background is totally different from mine, but I can identify with it psychologically. I'm not P.B., but I know him very well."[57]

This chapter begins recounting how P.B. Jones was abandoned as a baby in a St. Louis vaudeville theater, raised in a Missouri orphanage by Catholic nuns, one of whom recognized and encouraged his ability to write and convinced him he had a special gift, ran away from the orphanage at the age of fifteen and was picked up by a man in a white Cadillac convertible. P.B. calls himself a "Hershey Bar whore—there wasn't much I wouldn't do for a nickel's worth of chocolate."[58] The man who picked him up is a masseur in a Miami Beach hotel and teaches P.B. his trade. P.B. takes off for New York City, enrolls in a creative writing class at Columbia, marries a girl he met in his class, decides she is a moron and leaves her.

The fiction editor of a woman's fashion magazine comes to speak to the class at Columbia and P.B. can tell the man is attracted to him. He brings to the editor several short stories he has been writing, they have sex in the editor's office, the editor hesitantly offers to help P.B. get published and, after twenty submissions, buys one of his stories for publication. Through this editor, he meets a highly regarded author in her fifties, a woman of androgynous beauty who has had four husbands. P.B. and the author lives together, he becomes her protégé, and soon he begins receiving grants and fellowships, (P.B. "had drilled" her "till she geysered Guggenheims"),[59] an advance, her assistance in editing his stories, and her glowing review of his published collection of stories titled *Answered Prayers and Other Stories*, a title she selected: " ... the theme moving through your work, as nearly as I can locate it, is of people achieving a desperate aim only to have it rebound upon them—accentuating, and accelerating, their desperation."[60] The book upon publication is ignored: "My defeat, my cold hell."[61]

That is as far as his patroness can take him " ... for P.B. had already encountered the future. His name was Denham Fouts ... " Here Capote introduces Denny into the novel. "Denny, long before he surfaced in my cove, was a legend well-known to me, a myth entitled: Best-Kept Boy in the World."[62]

Capote recounts the saga of Denham Fouts, many of the details of his story adhering precisely to history, others introducing elements that may have been his elaborations, or Denny's, or may indeed have been part of the real story as told to him by Denny during their June days and nights together in Paris on that massive bed in Peter Watson's apartment.

As Capote tells the story in this chapter, Denny is working in a bakery owned by his father in a Florida "cracker town" when a cosmetics tycoon who has made a fortune on a "celebrated suntan lotion" spots him and takes him to Miami, and from there to Paris, and on to all the celebrated spots of Europe. On Capri, Denny "caught the eye of and absconded with a seventy-year-old-great-grandfather, who was also a director of Dutch Petroleum."[63] Prince Paul of Greece appears next and together "they visited a tattooist in Vienna and had themselves identically marked—a small blue insignia above the heart."[64] According to Capote's account, "women experimented with Denny: the Honorable Daisy Fellowes, the American Singer Sewing Machine heiress, lugged him around the Aegean aboard her crisp little yacht, the *Sister Anne*."[65]

In P.B.'s narrative, Denny in 1938 meets Peter Watson "his final and permanent patron" who he describes as "not just another rich queen, but—in a stooped, intellectual bitter-lipped style—one of the most personable men in England."[66]

Capote captures well the essence of his friend—"Denny was suited to only one role, The Beloved, for that was all he had ever been,"[67] and an insight into Denny's character: "One had to have experienced Denny's stranglehold, a pressure that brought the victim teasingly close to an ultimate slumber, to appreciate its allure."[68] Capote believed that "Watson was in love with Denny's cruelty ...The Beloved even used his drug addiction to sado-romantic advantage, for Watson, while forced to supply money that supported a habit he deplored, was convinced that only his love and attention could rescue The Beloved from a heroin grave. When The Beloved truly desired a turn of the screw, he had merely turn to his medicine chest."[69]

A tantalizing passage of the chapter describes just how P.B.—Capote—makes his way to Paris. P.B.'s first book had been published when he received a letter that read:

Dear Mr. Jones, Your stories are brilliant. So is Cecil Beaton's portrait. Please join me here as my guest. Enclosed is a first-class passage aboard the *Queen Elizabeth*, sailing New York-Le Havre April 24. If you require a reference, ask Beaton: he is an old acquaintance. Sincerely, Denham Fouts.[70]

P.B. realizes that it is not his book that Denham finds so captivating, but rather the photograph on the jacket of the book. "The photograph conveyed a notion of me altogether incorrect—a crystal lad, guileless, unsoiled, dewy, and sparkling as an April raindrop. Ho ho ho."[71]

P.B. arrives in Paris to find Denny "living in Watson's Paris apartment on a day-to-day squatter's-rights basis, and existing on scattered handouts from loyal friends and old, semi-blackmailed suitors."[72] To P.B., Denny appears "paler than his favorite ivory opium pipe," though "he still looked vulnerably young, as though youth were a chemical solution in which Fouts was permanently incarcerated."[73]

In an opium-induced reverie, Denny speaks to P.B. of the hopelessness he feels, the hopelessness that is at the heart of Capote's *Answered Prayers*, an existence that lay just on the far side of the "lives of quiet desperation" Thoreau attributed to most men:

> Tell me, boy, have you ever heard of Father Flanagan's Nigger Queen Kosher Café? Sound familiar? You betcher balls. Even if you never heard of it and maybe think it's some after hours Harlem dump, even so, you know it by *some* name, and of course you know what it is and where it is. Once I spent a year meditating in a California monastery. Under the supervision of His Holiness, the Right Reverend Mr. Gerald Heard. Looking for this ... Meaningful thing. This ... God Thing. I *did try*. No man was ever more naked. Early to bed and early to rise, and prayer, prayer, no hooch, no smokes, I never even jacked off. And all that ever came of that putrid torture was ... Father Flanagan's Nigger Queen Kosher Café.

Denny had told Capote all about his stay in California with Christopher Isherwood, of his experiences with Gerald Heard, the Swami, and Vedanta.

> There it is: right where they throw you off at the end of the line. Just beyond the garbage dump ... Now knock. Knock knock. Father Flanagan's voice: "Who sent ya?" Christ, for Christ's sake, ya dumb mick.

Inside ... it's ... very ... relaxing. Because there's not a winner in the crowd ... So you can really unpin your hair, Cinderella. And admit that what we have here is the drop-off. What a relief! Just to throw in the cards, order a Coke, and take a spin around the floor with an old friend ... The Nigger Queen Kosher Café! The cool, green, restful as the grave, rock bottom! That's why I drug: mere dry meditation isn't enough to get me there, keep me there, hidden and happy with Father Flanagan and his Outcast of Thousands, him and all the other yids, nigs, spiks, fags, dykes, dope fiends, and commies. Happy to be down there where you belong: Yassah, massuh! Except—the price is too high. I'm killing myself.[74]

Denny finds a new friend in P.B., and, as always with a new friendship comes a renewed interest in life. "I wouldn't object to living," he tells P.B., "provided you lived with me, Jonesy," then spinning his fantasy of together buying a filling station in Arizona or Nevada: "It would be real quiet, and you could write stories. Basically, I'm pretty healthy. I'm a good cook, too."[75]

Just as Capote did with Fouts, P.B. convinces Denny to go to a Swiss clinic, with the promise to meet in Positano or Ravello once his treatment is complete, though " ...I had no intention of doing so, or of seeing Denny again if it could be avoided."[76]

With Denny in the rehabilitation clinic, P.B. returns to New York City, trying again to write, now working on a novel he titled *Answered Prayers*, just like the title of his collection of short stories that had sold but three hundred copies. He is at rock bottom, penniless, feeling his dream of a writing career drifting from him. At the Central Park Zoo, he meets an old friend, "the descendant of our twenty-eighth President," who, seeing that P.B. is down and out, tells him how he and a Yale friend of his who is a stock broker and trying to put his two sons through Exeter are making extra money by hustling, hired out by the hour by a Miss Self who runs a service from an office on Forty-second Street. P.B. signs up as an employee, and his first customer that afternoon is Mr. Wallace, an "acclaimed American playwright" (Tennessee Williams) staying at the Plaza Hotel with his English bulldog.

Some weeks later, P.B. receives a note from Denny to call him. When P.B. reaches him, Denny tells him that he is ready to leave the clinic, and suggests that they meet in Rome where a friend has lent him an apartment. P.B. agrees, but he has no intention of meeting, "for how could I say I never meant to see him again because he scared me? It wasn't the drugs and chaos but the funereal halo of waste and failure seemed somehow to threaten my own impending triumph."[77] For P.B. was at work now on another novel—*Sleepless Millions*—which he felt sure would be recognized as a masterpiece, all the while supporting himself by working for Miss Self. After a session with yet another customer, he "began to remember Denny Fouts and to wish I could dash downstairs and find a bus, the Magic Mushroom Express, a chartered torpedo that would rocket me to the end of the line, zoom me all the way to the halcyon discotheque: Father Flanagan's Nigger Queen Kosher Café."[78]

Capote's opening chapter, "Unspoiled Monster," set a dark tone for what promised to be a disturbing novel. A third chapter from his work in progress, "Kate McCloud," was published in *Esquire* in December of 1976. And that was it. There would be no more chapters published. Ever. Nothing more would ever be seen of *Answered Prayers*.

On several occasions as the years passed, he announced that the manuscript was complete and that Random House would publish it within six months, but his editors never received a page more than the three chapters published in *Esquire*.

There was evidence that he had written a lot more. One

day he was visiting John Knowles at his home in Nyack and had brought with him what he said was the manuscript of *Answered Prayers*. "He started to show it to me. There was a lot of it, much more than has been published. Much more than has ever been found. I said, 'Oh, later,' which was madness on my part because he was making a great concession by showing me something of a work in progress. He never offered to show it to me again. I'm absolutely certain that he wrote a great deal more of that book."[79] His good friend Joanne Carson, former wife of Johnny Carson, had read three long chapters, "The Nigger Queen Kosher Café," "Yachts and Things," and "And Audrey Wilder Sang," which have never been found. Other friends had been with Capote at dinners when he entertained them by reciting unpublished chapters from memory, just as he had done when writing *In Cold Blood*.

Capote admitted that "I did stop working on *Answered Prayers* in September 1977,"[80] explaining that he had re-read not only the early chapters of his novel-in-progress but also each book and story he had written, and realized that all could be better. "Slowly, but with accelerating alarm, I read every word I'd ever published, and decided that never, not once in my writing life, had I completely exploded all the energy and esthetic excitements that material contained. Even when it was good, I could see that I was never working with more than half, sometimes only a third, of the powers at my command."[81] That conclusion may have resulted in a massive writer's block that stopped any more work.

Capote called *Answered Prayers* "the *raison d'etre* of my entire life."[82] What had gone wrong? Had he set the bar too high? Was he over-thinking what he was doing? Had his society friends' stormy reactions so thrown him off his game that his vision of the book was destroyed? Or did he complete his manuscript, with the whereabouts of its remaining chapters the mystery of twentieth century literature?

John Knowles remembered how Capote had been talking with him for years about his work on the manuscript "in a way which I'm sure was authentic. He said, 'It's absorbing everything, it's taking in everything.' Then one day at McCarthy's restaurant in Southampton, Truman said to me, 'I've been working, working, working, working, and you know, sometimes you look back at your work and you see that it just isn't any good.' I think he had come to that point. Whether he was right or wrong about his own work, I don't know. I think he burned hundreds and hundreds of pages because he thought they weren't any good."[83]

He was staying with Joanne Carson the day he died, August 25, 1984, at the age of fifty-nine.

"Truman," Joanne had asked him that day, "what happened to *Answered Prayers*; it's not finished yet?"

"Oh, yes it is," she recalled him saying.

"How will anybody know where or how to find them [the remaining chapters] if something happens to you?"

"Don't worry, they will be found when they are ready to be found."

"But you know there are a lot of people who say you never finished *Answered Prayers*. If something happens to you and these aren't found, people are not going to be convinced."

Truman started talking about a safe deposit box.

"Where? What bank? What city?" Joanne asked.

"Well, they could be on Long Island, in Manhattan, or they could be in Palm Springs, or maybe they're in San Francisco. Or maybe right here in Los Angeles. Texas, even New Orleans."

He gave the safe deposit key to Joanne Carson that day, and later she gave it to Alan Schwartz, his lawyer and executor. "We could never find the safe-deposit box," Schwartz reported. There was a key, and we tried to track it everywhere. We couldn't. So we're left with that."[84]

In the three chapters of Capote's novel-in-progress

published in *Esquire*, what may have become two of his most memorable characters are just beginning to emerge: P.B. and Kate McCloud, a sophisticated young beauty who hires P.B. to be her "masseuse." An underlying theme running through the three chapters is that life is such that everyone does what they have to do to get along—from Denny Fouts to P.B., to the fourteen- and fifteen-year-old male hustlers P.B. passed late one night as he walked to the movies ("Mister! Ten dollars! Take me home! Fuck me all night!"),[85] to the Wall Streeter who becomes an employee of Miss Self to make some extra money to put his sons through Exeter. And doing what they have to do to make their lives work, maybe everything will turn out alright: maybe the Wall Streeter's sons will get through Exeter and accepted at Harvard, maybe the teenage hustlers will find their way, maybe the novel P.B. is working on will be the masterpiece he hopes. But maybe not. And that maybe not is what looms behind the three extant chapters. To Capote, that maybe not is exemplified in Denham Fouts, and it is therefore not surprising that he planned the last chapter of his novel to be "The Nigger Queen Kosher Café."

In his notes, Capote considered "The Nigger Queen Kosher Café" the climax of the book. Here, perhaps, Denny Fouts who had introduced the idea of this dead end depository in "Unspoiled Monsters," would have appeared again, and if so, it is likely that Capote considered Denny a key character, his story a unifying theme, a motif of the book, representing that end-of-the line world of those who life has beaten, who never find their way, their place in the world, who have lost hope and all their dreams.

Capote's own life, hauntingly, had followed the theme of his novel-in-progress, line and verse: his prayers had been answered with the overwhelming success of *In Cold Blood* and when those hopes became reality, "more tears were shed." His life had death-spiraled in the very way that had frightened him so during those blissful June days in Paris in 1948 when his own world was so full of promise, when he had stayed with Denham Fouts and seen him at the bottom—an addict about to be evicted from Peter Watson's apartment—sensing then just how easily such a bottom could be his own, or anyone's, lot.

CHAPTER EIGHT

"I'M SICK OF MORALIZATIONS"

Truman Capote was among the last who came to visit Denny as the noose tightened around his life. Whether in reality or in his mind, the gendarmes seemed to be closing in, both because of his purchase of drugs and his penchant for handsome teenagers. It would just be days before he was forcibly evicted from Peter's apartment.

Denny decided to move to Rome when he heard that heroin could be obtained easily there and learned from Gore Vidal that the police in Rome let the trade in rent boys flourish. He asked Michael Wishart to join him. "With a shudder of the soul," Michael knew that he no longer could be a part of Denny's life, that what he would look back on decades later when he wrote his memoirs as "the impurest happiness I have ever known"[1] was over. Denny accused Michael of cowardice, and left for Rome with Trotsky and Tony Watson-Gandy, the British RAF officer who adored him. There was always someone.

Michael returned alone to England. He never again would hear from Denny. Romantic passion triggers the same chemical reactions associated with all addictions, and in Michael's dopamine-drenched brain "the thought of Denham was painful for a long time"[2] as he suffered through the throes of withdrawal.

I'M SICK OF MORALIZATIONS

The poet Charles Henri Ford, who for over two decades was the lover of Pavel Tchelitchev, the artist who had painted that huge Adonis nude that had hung above Denny's bed in Paris, wrote in his diary in September of 1948 that a friend had told him that Denham at thirty-four "still looks so young, not over 28, no lines in his face, hasn't got a gray hair." Ford noted in his diary that "it's not doing the things one wants to do—even if considered a 'vice,' like opium taking—that makes one age, but doing the things one *doesn't* want to do."[3] Denny continued on as he always had, trying not to do the things he didn't want to do. It was getting harder.

From Rome, Denny wrote increasingly desperate letters to Peter Watson, alternatively asking for money and accusing him of causing all his problems. Peter was facing his own problems. His income from the trust funds had fallen sharply, taxes in England had risen, and his investments in France had been wiped out by the War. As Waldemar Hansen wrote about Peter to a friend on September 11, 1948: "And now, he's reduced to watching the lira in Italy, eating in cautious style, etc. He can't buy any more paintings because he hasn't got the money abroad, and England won't import. He loathes London and has to live there most of the time. He hasn't got a car, nor a house, nor an apartment in Paris. He watches the area of his life get smaller and smaller and smaller."[4]

Peter was well aware how his life had changed: "I seem to have suffered the death of feeling myself," he had written to a friend a few months before:

I just can't react any more. It all seems so futile anyway, as we are under the sentence of death, I feel. If only the world contained some hope. Intelligence, freedom are monstrous luxuries which this world can no longer afford. If only I could take things for granted like any stupid person can ... Like you, I am only interested in life it if reaches a certain standard,

146

and now that standard has gone forever and there is no pleasure left which is not ersatz ... How terrible it is to grow old. One loses so many tastes one had and seems to get no new ones at all. Wisdom doesn't settle anything—it only removes one from old friends and prevents one from making any new ones. Then it is so humiliating to have all one's old beliefs and enthusiasms turned inside out. The only thing is to be young as it makes egotism elegant.[5]

Peter once remarked to a friend that "I cannot bear to see self-destruction in friends or in anyone else, and I react violently against it."[6] Watching from afar as Denny's life careened out of control made him miserable.

Peter knew that Denny was "diabolical in pinning the blame on to others,"[7] but nevertheless was tormented by his letters, and on November 30 wrote to Waldemar: "Denham wrote me a reproachful self-pitying letter from Rome saying that I had done nothing to help him! My God, I have been paying for all his self-indulgent auto-destruction, besides his doctors and nursing homes ... I can't understand what people want of me or expect me to do. Denham and what happened to him is the perfect example of someone evading every issue through someone else, and when he does have to stand on his own legs, they just aren't there. So he is forced to use everyone else as a prop to his own weakness."[8]

Johnny Goodwin, a wealthy American author who Denny had befriended in California, visited him in Rome in November. "He and Denny are like brothers," Christopher Isherwood commented, "in many ways, Johnny is simply Denny with money." Denny, though, was wary of his friend's visit: "You can sit here as long as you don't start moralizing," Denny told him. "I'm sick of moralizations."[9] Like everyone else, Johnny tried reasoning. As he wrote to Christopher:

147

... I told him very brutally why he had lost all his friends (as he constantly complained of), it was that he was not himself any more. He asked in his strange, rational and yet hazy way just in what way was he different. It was hard to tell him for I meant really saying that he was not at all rational, that his habits of lying abed and living a kind of Poe existence made it difficult to share anything of the world with him. But he seemed to see finally what I meant and for a week until I left, though his habits didn't change, he wanted to live, which was something he hadn't cared one way or another about for a long time. He was seriously considering going to England or America to a psychiatrist which I was all for, even though I admitted to him and he agreed that they were only a very last resort.[10]

According to Denny's cousin, Denny was planning to return to the United States, home to Jacksonville to write. He sent ahead to his mother a large mailing envelope stuffed with manuscript pages—perhaps a draft of his memoirs. His mother read them, realized her son was gay, and burned every page.[11]

Bernard Perlin, a young artist who had met Denny in Rome, visited Denny early in December, Denny in bed, corpse-like, the sheet drawn to his chin, a cigarette between his lips, his lover, Tony, removing the cigarette and tapping it each time before it burned him. This was to be his final visitor. Ever a night fiend, Denny injected the drugs he kept in a cigar box in his room and, as always, instantly came to life, went out for the evening, and vaporized into the mists.[12]

On Christmas Day, December 25, 1948, Glenway Wescott sat in Stone-Blossom, his farm in Hampton, New Jersey, and in his perfect script, wrote to his friend, Christopher Isherwood, in Santa Monica, California:

I'M SICK OF MORALIZATIONS

Dear Christopher,

Christmas greetings, to begin with—and to Billy [Caskey] likewise.

But I am a notable customary Scrooge, and this is to tell bad pitiful news. Denham is dead—Thursday evening the 16th.

My friend, Bernard Perlin has been staying in the same pensione; went away to the mountains to make some sketches for *Fortune*, and returning Friday night or Saturday morning, found Denham's friend Tony overwhelmed with all the nightmarish duties, autopsy that day, kindly but bothering police, burial, etc.—and as of that date had not notified anyone; found no proper address book, no line of communication to the parents.

So this morning I ... find it in my heart to write this to you first, saying to myself that it would give you a more desolate feeling if you heard it still later, still farther round-about. If it is superfluous, if it seems officious—forgive me; put it down to my own sorrowfulness, not great but true & peculiar, of the many years, fourteen years.

Note that it was not the worst death—he went to the bathroom and did not return, ten or fifteen minutes passed—he had fallen to the floor; apparently a simple and instant heart failure.[13]

As he wrote to Isherwood, and a day or two later when he wrote in his journal, Wescott pondered the news, for "I was one of the first of the elders-edifiers-influencers in his

149

accursed life,"[14] having instructed him in the art of attracting the right admirers. For the fourteen years he had known him, Wescott had always been vaguely troubled by the role he had played in Denham's life. In his letter to Christopher, Glenway began to ruminate about his first encounters with Denny:

> Come to think of it, I know what impels me to write to you. When we spoke of him that evening at Lincoln's [Kirstein], it gave me goose-flesh—as in the ancient sense of the word, panic—I told you then, didn't I? How he used to come to me, in the spring of 1934, and inquire (as of a like but elder Rubempre or Rastignac) how to pursue his fortune, how to maneuver his youth in the great world—and oh, what was ever great about it! And though I would wring my hands at concepts of himself & of life overall already fixed in his stubborn young head, though I would mildly scold and altruistically argue, I have always looked back on it uneasily, wondering . . .

Glenway was able to end his account with a report that, to the end, Denny was Denny:

> Bernard met him for the first time there in the Pensione Foggette—and you will be pleased to know that he speaks of him as "very gentle, sweet, and for the better as for the worse, not grown-up."[15]

Denny had left no address book, but the word began to spread: after a lifetime of living way beyond the edge, Denham had died of a malformed heart, a ticking time bomb that could have taken him at any time.

Still in Rome, Johnny Goodwin was mystified and saddened. "I can't say what made Denny click. I can only say what his effect was on other people. He had great, great charm, and you always had the feeling that potentially he was something much more than he was."[16] Bill Harris, who had known Denny in California, said of Denny that "he thought that the world was made up of whores. To be a successful whore was all, he said. Though he didn't brag, he felt he had done pretty well at it."[17]

Peter Watson learned the news by telegram from Rome. On December 20, he wrote to Waldemar Hansen: "My own feelings are so mixed that I cannot begin to express them in a letter." A week later, a few days before he was to sail for the United States, he again wrote to Hansen as the news took hold of him: "Denham's death has affected me rather deeply. Please be very patient with me because I shall arrive in a very depressed condition."[18]

After seeing to Denny's burial, Tony Watson-Gandy packed up his belongings from the apartment he shared with Denny and, with Trotsky, returned to England to his family's estate.

Denny was buried in the Protestant Cemetery in Rome. He would have been delighted with the company. John Keats, the young English poet, had come to Rome in 1820, seeking a cure from tuberculosis, and there, long "before my pen has glean'd my teeming brain," died the next year at the age of twenty-five. His tombstone identified him only as a "YOUNG ENGLISH POET." Despairing over the critical reception of his poems, Keats had asked there be inscribed on his stone these words: "Here lies One whose Name was writ in Water." No name need have been inscribed, for his output in an eighteen month period of white-hot inspiration before his death secured his position as an immortal, and forever after, visitors have come to the Protestant Cemetery, a place of pilgrimage, to pay homage. Indeed, when in Rome in the Spring of 1877, Oscar Wilde had an audience with Pope Pius IX, and later the same day visited the Protestant Cemetery. It was this cemetery, not the Vatican, that he called "the holiest place in Rome," for here lay the remains of that "divine boy," John Keats. Wilde fell to his knees in reverence in front of the headstone, something he had not done at the Vatican.[19]

Percy Bysshe Shelley, in his preface to "Adonais," his long elegy to his fallen friend, wrote a year after Keats died that "it might make one in love with death to know that one should be buried in so sweet a place." And buried there Shelley was the following year, when this other young English Romantic poet drowned on July 8, 1822 while sailing in a storm in the Gulf of Spezia off Livorno, Tuscany.

Keats. Shelly. Richard Henry Dana, the author of *Two Years Before the Mast*. Antonio Gramsci, the founder of the Italian Communist party. Here on this hilly five acre oasis off the Via Ciao Cesio, near Porta San Paola, surrounded in part by a section of the forty foot high Aurelian Wall built in the third century to keep the barbarians from Rome, shadowed by the ninety-foot, marble-clad pyramid built in the first century by the Roman magistrate Gaius Cestus, who was enthralled with all things Egyptian, here, amid the ancient Mediterranean cypress and pines, lay sculptors, artists, a Beat generation poet, philosophers, diplomats.

Today, the gray walls that "moulder round," as Shelley wrote, dim the bustle of the city, the noise of traffic and trains and the nearby factories and car repair shops of the Testaccio district. Cats scamper and drape themselves over grieving marble angels or doze on headstones or lead the occasional visitor around the paths of this dreamy, lush sanctuary with the look of an Italian garden with its overgrown flowering trees and shrubs and crumbling Victorian monuments.

Michael Wishart found himself ringing the bell for the custodian at the gates of the Protestant Cemetery. He had come to say goodbye to his friend who had brought "pure joy"[20] to his life, who had given him the happiest days, weeks, and months he would ever experience. As he wandered alone along the forlorn paths, he saw none of the evocative beauty of the spot which had so entranced Shelley. To Michael, it was bleak and forbidding, with the old cypress trees casting cold shadows over Denny's grave, a grave which seemed to him "forsaken, separated from the rest."[21] The United States Consulate had been unable to locate any family member when Denny died in Rome, and so paid for his burial in the south side of the cemetery, near the grave of Keats.[22]

Michael stared at that twenty-three inch by forty inch marble headstone:

LOUIS DENHAM FOUTS + 16 DEC. 1948

"The sight of his name chiseled into stone made me feel violently sick. I tried to visualize what remained, a mere few metres beneath my feet. What had become of the scorpion tattooed in his groin that I had kissed so many times?"[23] And as he looked and remembered and heard in the breeze through the cypress his deep Southern drawl—we had fun, didn't we? those were good times—Michael wished he could lay a blanket of primroses over the grave, just as, so many times before, he had pulled the covers up to Denny's chin.

Like the ghost of Jimmie Trimble, Denny's presence always hovered about those who had loved him.

Glenway Wescott in early March of 1949 traveled to California for a short vacation and stayed in a hotel in Santa Monica close to Christopher Isherwood's home. After a visit with Isherwood, Wescott wrote to praise a manuscript of his he had just finished reading, adding to his letter a parenthetical: "(By the way, sorry to have aroused your grief about D.—how ever did I happen to?—sorry, sorry. But no regret—you must sometimes grieve uninhibitedly—let blood wash the cut.)"[24]

Later that month, Peter Watson visited Christopher Isherwood, and Christopher and Bill Caskey took Peter to a bar "the Gala, because it was such a haunt of Denny's. It was almost empty, and very sad."[25]

When Dylan Thomas was in California in December of

1953 to give a reading at UCLA, he stopped to visit Isherwood. "When I showed him my workroom, he at once noticed Denny's photograph on the wall and said respectfully, 'He's very beautiful.' I felt quite sorry that I had to explain the mistake," Christopher noted in his diary.[26]

Two years later, on November 14, 1955, "the most marvelous Indian summer" day, Christopher stopped in Tivoli during his travels through Italy. "We went to Denny's grave in the Protestant Cemetery," he wrote in his diary, "and I cried. It all seemed such a wretched tangle—his life, and mine too. I'm depressed here ...Europe, in its autumn, reminds me of my own. And I seem to myself to look older every day. And I feel no ripening, no resignation. I don't want to get old or die."[27]

Four years later, on November 16, 1959, Isherwood had lunch with Aldous Huxley who told Christopher about taking mescaline and the spiritual experiences it promoted. One involved a dream about Denny, which he described. "He saw Denny naked, on a horse. Riding along a precipice road, bounded by a cliff. There was a door in the cliff, into a cave. The horse threw Denny and he banged through the door and fell into the cave. He was very badly hurt. One of his legs twitched uncontrollably. He crawled back out of the cave on to the road and collapsed. Aldous was bending over him with extreme concern and compassion; then Aldous woke."[28]

But Denny remained more real than a presence in ephemeral conversations and memories and dreams. He never did write his memoirs, but in living his life on his own terms he created a work of art that inspired others.

Michael Wishart knew that Denny was pleased to have been the inspiration for a character in Somerset Maugham's novel *The Razor's Edge*, Sophie, "the hopelessly self-destructive opiumaniac drunken girl";[29] Wishart noted that the novelist "had been fascinated by Denham" and modeled this character who bought her opium in Toulon, just as Denny did, after him, "of which Denham was strangely proud."[30] No doubt, he would have been proud, too, that his best friend, Christopher Isherwood, immortalized him as Paul in *Down There on a Visit*, that Gore Vidal, who had known him for but a few weeks, had preserved him in amber in *The Judgment of Paris* and as Elliott in "Pages From an Abandoned Journal," that Truman Capote was so captivated by him to bring him to life as himself in "Unspoiled Monsters." Denny had exchanged what he realized was the fleetingness of mortality for the eternity of art, continuing to live on with an actuality greater than most people had while alive.

Like Ulysses in Tennyson's poem, Denny well understood how "that which we are, we are." Like the Greek hero, he had drunk life to the lees: "All times I have enjoyed/Greatly, have suffered greatly, both with those/That loved me, and alone." And with the ancient wanderer, he too, could say that "always roaming with a hungry heart/Much have I seen and known."

Like Ulysses, Denham Fouts had "become a name."

"I am a part of all that I have met," Tennyson wrote of Ulysses. Denny became a part of everyone who knew him. And to become a part of a writer is perhaps as close to immortality as anyone can get.

NOTES

FOREWORD

1. Vidal, *Palimpsest*, p. 180, p. 179.
2. Clarke, *Capote*, p. 173.
3. Rorem, *A Ned Rorem Reader*, p. 275.
4. Clarke, pp. 171-172.
5. Vidal, p. 180. Plimpton, *Truman Capote*, p. 88.
6. Clarke, p. 172.
7. Wishart, *High Diver*, p. 52.
8. Clarke, p. 172.

CHAPTER ONE

1. Shelden, *Friends of Promise*, p. 180, p. 29.
2. Shelden, p. 132.
3. Lewis, *Cyril Connolly*, p. 395.
4. Shelden, p. 133.
5. Lewis, p. 395.
6. Wishart, *High Diver*, p. 18.
7. Ibid., p. 21.
8. Ibid.
9. Ibid., p. 19.
10. Ibid., p. 22.
11. Ibid.
12. Spender, *World Within World*, p. 266.

13. Wishart, p. 25.
14. Ibid.
15. Ibid., p. 49.
16. Ibid., p. 50.
17. Ibid. pp. 50-51.
18. Ibid., p. 51.
19. Ibid.
20. Ibid.
21. Ibid., p. 52.
22. Ibid.
23. Ibid.
24. Ibid.
25. Ibid., p. 53.
26. Ibid.
27. Wishart, p. 53.
28. Shelden, p. 181.
29. Ibid.
30. Ibid.
31. Ibid.
32. Ibid., p. 53.
33. Ibid., p. 54.
34. Ibid., p. 54.
35. Ibid., p. 57.
36. Ibid., p. 57.
37. Ibid., p. 56.
38. Ibid.
39. Ibid., p. 57.
40. Ibid., p. 60.
41. Ibid., p. 60.
42. Ibid., p. 54.
43. Ibid., p. 54
44. Lewis, p. 405.
45. Wishart, p. 60.

NOTES

CHAPTER TWO

1. Phelps and Rosco, *Continual Lessons*, p. 59.
2. Clarke, *Capote*, p. 172.
3. Plimpton, *Truman Capote*, p. 87.

CHAPTER THREE

1. Pryce-Jones, *The Bonus of Laughter*, p. 31.
2. Price-Jones, *Cyril Connolly*, p. 136.
3. Murray, *Aldous Huxley*, p. 91.
4. Bell, *The Diary of Virginia Woolf*, pp. 78-79.
5. Pryce-Jones, *The Bonus of Laughter*, p. 31.
6. Ibid.
7. Graves and Hodge, *The Long Weekend*, p. 114.
8. Lancaster, *Brian Howard*, p. 101.
9. Murray, pp. 100-101.
10. Benkovitz, *Ronald Firbank*, p. 125.
11. Ibid., p. 181.
12. Taylor, *Bright Young People*, p. 286.
13. Benkovitz, p. 110.
14. Ibid., p. 112.
15. Ibid., p. 189.
16. Taylor, p. 232.
17. Benkovitz, p. 182.
18. Ibid.
19. Ibid., p. 189.
20. Pryce-Jones, *The Bonus of Laughter*, p. 30.
21. Ibid., p. 31.
22. Taylor, p. 232.
23. Benkovitz, p. 249.
24. Plimpton, *Truman Capote*, p. 88.

25. Murray, p. 166.
26. Pryce-Jones, *The Bonus of Laughter*, 32-33.
27. Plimpton, p. 88.
28. Pryce-Jones, *The Bonus of Laughter*, p. 33.
29. Ibid., p. 31.
30. Ibid., p. 31.
31. Montgomery-Massingberd, *Great Houses of England and Wales*, p. 209.
32. Kaczynski, *Perdurabo*, p. 435.
33. Montgomery-Massingberd, p. 212.
34. Wishart, *High Diver*, p. 52.
35. Richard Wall, "The World's Most Expensive Male Prostitute," *Folio Weekly* (Jacksonville, Florida), June 12, 2012.

CHAPTER FOUR

1. Pryce-Jones, *The Bonus of Laughter*, p. 29.
2. Buckle, *Self Portrait with Friends*, p. 27.
3. Ibid., p. 304.
4. Goldsmith, *Stephen Spender Journals*, p. 160.
5. Shelden, *Friends of Promises*, p.32.
6. Buckle, p. 305.
7. Beaton, *The Wandering Years*, p. 270.
8. Buckle, p. 304.
9. Ibid., p. 305.
10. Vickers, *Cecil Beaton*, p. 149.
11. Beaton, p. 222.
12. Vickers, p. 150.
13. Ibid., p. 151.
14. Ibid.
15. Ibid., p. 152.
16. Ibid., p. 155.

17. Ibid., p. 160.
18. Capote, *Answered Prayers*, p. 27.
19. Vickers, p. 160.
20. Ibid., p. 222.
21. Shelden, p. 181.
22. Ibid., p. 32.
23. Vickers, p. 175.
24. Ibid., p. 167.
25. Ibid.
26. Vickers, p. 397.
27. Wishart, *High Diver*, p. 49.
28. Shelden, p. 181.
29. Vickers, p. 148.
30. Shelden, p. 181.
31. Ibid., p. 117.
32. Ibid., p. 181.
33. Ibid.
34. Ibid.
35. Vickers, p. 397.
36. Shelden, p. 181.
37. Rorem, *A Ned Rorem Reader*, p. 275.
38. Geiger, *Nothing is True Everything is Permitted*, p. 47.
39. Ibid., p. 50.
40. Bowles, *Without Stopping*, p. 211.
41. *The Times*, London, October 22, 1988, Anne Campbell Dixon "Spurning the Suit of Paint Strictures: Interview with John Craxton".
42. Sutherland, *Stephen Spender*, p. 387.
43. Goldsmith, p. 434.
44. Shelden, p. 180.
45. Ibid., p. 30.
46. Undated letter from Peter Watson to Cecil Beaton in Beaton Archives.
47. Shelden, p. 180, p. 29.
48. Cyril Connolly Papers, 1938.

49. Fisher, *Cyril Connolly*, p. 174.
50. Shelden, p. 33.
51. Fisher, p. 183.
52. *The Guardian*, Feb. 11, 1989, Stephen Spender, "Waiting for Bombers".
53. Spender, *World Within World*, p. 240.
54. Phelps and Rosco, *Continual Lessons*, p. 59.
55. Letter of Peter Watson to Cecil Beaton, Papers of Cecil Beaton, Wednesday, Summer 1940 from Thatched Cottage Thurlestons Sands, South Devon.
56. Shelden, p. 41.
57. Lewis, *Cyril Connolly*, p. 332.
58. *Christian Science Monitor*, Dec. 11, 1989, Merle Rubin, "Horizon: Wartime Magazine that Kept Culture Afloat".
59. Spender, *The Thirties and After*, p. 66.

CHAPTER FIVE

1. Bucknell, *Christopher Isherwood: Lost Years: A Memoir*, p. 4.
2. Parker, *Isherwood: A Life Revealed*, p. 359.
3. Ibid., p. 375.
4. Murray, *Aldous Huxley*, p. 253.
5. Ibid., p. 377.
6. Ibid., p. 378.
7. Lewis, *Cyril Connolly: A Life*, p. 380.
8. Bucknell, *Christopher Isherwood Diaries: Volume One: 1939-1960*, p. 118.
9. Lewis, p. 380.
10. Bucknell, *Christopher Isherwood Diaries*, p. 118.
11. Isherwood, *My Guru and His Disciple*, pp. 59-60.
12. Berg and Freeman, *Conversations with Christopher Isherwood*, p. 187.

13. Bucknell, *Christopher Isherwood Diaries*, p. 118.
14. Bucknell, *Christopher Isherwood: Lost Years*, p. 222; Finney, *Christopher Isherwood: A Critical Biography*, p. 226.
15. Isherwood, *Down There on a Visit*, pp. 185-186.
16. Ibid., p. 186.
17. Ibid., p. 184.
18. Ibid., p. 187.
19. Parker, p. 594.
20. Isherwood, *My Guru and His Disciple*, p. 60.
21. Isherwood, *Down There on a Visit*, p. 196.
22. Ibid., p. 198.
23. Ibid., p. 202.
24. Ibid., p. 203.
25. Ibid., p. 204.
26. Ibid.
27. Ibid., p. 207.
28. Ibid., p. 209.
29. Ibid.
30. Ibid., p. 210.
31. Ibid.
32. Ibid., p. 211.
33. Ibid., p. 231.
34. Ibid., p. 229.
35. Ibid.
36. Ibid., p. 240.
37. Ibid., p. 246.
38. Ibid.
39. Ibid., p. 253.
40. Ibid., p. 268.
41. Ibid., p. 270.
42. Ibid., p. 276.
43. Ibid., p. 292.
44. Ibid., p. 294.
45. Ibid., p. 295.

46. Ibid.
47. Ibid., p. 296.
48. Ibid., p. 298.
49. Ibid., p. 299.
50. Finney, pp. 243-244.
51. Ibid., p. 235.
52. Berg and Freeman, p. 187. Isherwood, in June of 1961, gave the manuscript of *Down There On a Visit* to Truman Capote to read. Capote told a friend that he "liked it *very* much. Sort of 'Goodbye to Berlin' brought up to date. It's almost *too* frank." Clarke, *Too Brief a Treat*, p. 321.
53. Bucknell, *Christopher Isherwood Diaries*, pp. 122-123.
54. Ibid., p. 123.
55. Isherwood, *My Guru and His Disciple*, p. 61.
56. Ibid., p. 61.
57. Bucknell, *Christopher Isherwood Diaries*, p. 123.
58. Ibid., p. 144.
59. Parker, p. 452.
60. Isherwood, *My Guru and His Disciple*, p. 62.
61. Ibid., p. 84.
62. Ibid., p. 82.
63. Bucknell, *Christopher Isherwood Diaries*, p. 172.
64. Ibid, p. 171.
65. Isherwood, *My Guru and His Disciple*, p. 82.
66. Ibid., p. 83.
67. Ibid.
68. Isherwood, *Down There on a Visit*, p. 239.
69. Isherwood, *My Guru and His Disciple*, p. 161.
70. Parker, p. 425.
71. Bucknell, *Christopher Isherwood Diaries*, p. 156.
72. Ibid., p. 140.
73. Isherwood, *My Guru and His Disciple*, pp. 83-84.
74. Ibid., p. 85.
75. Ibid., p. 86.
76. Ibid., p. 85.

77. Ibid., p. 85.
78. Ibid., p. 86. Denham Fouts' notebooks are with the Christopher Isherwood Papers.
79. Denham Fouts' draft novel is with the Christopher Isherwood Papers.
80. Robert Louis Stevenson, "My First Book—Treasure Island"; foreword to *Treasure Island*, New York: Charles Scribner's Sons, 1902, pp. x-xi.
81. Bucknell, *Christopher Isherwood Diaries*, p. 180.
82. Ibid., p. 232.
83. Ibid., p. 274.
84. Ibid.
85. Ibid., p. 348.
86. Ibid., p. 352.
87. Finney, pp. 184-185.
88. Isherwood, *My Guru and His Disciple*, p. 180.
89. Bucknell, *Christopher Isherwood: Lost Years*, p. 10.
90. Bucknell, *Christopher Isherwood Diaries*, p. 297.
91. Ibid., p. 254.
92. Bucknell, *Christopher Isherwood: Lost Years*, p. 13.
93. Isherwood, *My Guru and His Disciple*, p. 179.
94. Bucknell, *Christopher Isherwood Diaries*, p. 316.
95. Ibid., p. 314.
96. Ibid., p. 158.
97. Parker, p. 474.
98. Bucknell, *Christopher Isherwood Diaries*, p. 341-342.
99. Ibid., p. 349.
100. Shelden, *Friends of Promise*, p. 58.
101. Bucknell, *Christopher Isherwood: Lost Years*, p. 212.
102. Ibid., p. 35.
103. Ibid., p. 40.
104. Isherwood, *My Guru and His Disciple*, pp. 136-137.
105. Isherwood, *Christopher Isherwood: Lost Years*, p. 18.
106. Ibid., p. 6.
107. Ibid., p. 19.

108. Ibid., p. 32.
109. Ibid., p. xvi; p. 275.
110. Ibid., p. 46.
111. Christopher Isherwood Papers, The Huntington Library, San Marino, California.
112. Bucknell, *Christopher Isherwood: Lost Years*, p. 69.
113. Ibid., p. 70.
114. Berg and Freeman, pp. 186-187.
115. Isherwood, *Down There on a Visit*, p. 31

CHAPTER SIX

1. Plimpton, *Truman Capote*, pp. 87-88.
2. Hibbard, *Paul Bowles Magic & Morocco*, p. 68.
3. Symonds, *The Beast 666*, pp. 566-567.
4. Unpublished Diaries of Aleister Crowley, p. 20.
5. Shelden, *Friends of Promise*, p. 116.
6. Papers of Cecil Beaton, undated letter of Peter Watson to Beaton.
7. Papers of Cecil Beaton, undated letter of Peter Watson to Beaton.
8. Shelden, p. 181.
9. Ibid., p. 58.
10. Ibid., p. 59.
11. Ibid.
12. Shelden, p. 179.
13. Ibid., p. 180. As described by Michel Shelden in *Friends of Promise*, the two in early June left London for Paris, road bicycles around the city each day, "visited Museums and Watson's favourite galleries, and in the evenings they almost always went out—to plays, nightclubs, or even the opera. They ate at the best restaurants ...At the end of June they went to the South of France and spent July there in

Cannes, Nice, and Monte Carlo. August found them in Switzerland, Florence, Rome and Capri. Early in September they were back in Paris for several days, then returned to London. "I haven't got much to say about love yet," Hansen wrote to a friend in September, "I'm too busy relaxing in it." (pp. 184-185). Hansen had a poem published in *Horizon* in May, reviewed books for the publication and served as editorial reader.

14. Ibid., p. 181.
15. Vidal, *Palimpsest*, pp. 25, 26.
16. Ibid., p. 82.
17. Ibid., p. 29-30.
18. Ibid., p. 83.
19. Ibid., p. 31.
20. Ibid., p. 281.
21. Ibid., p. 27.
22. Kaplan, *Gore Vidal*, p. 785.
23. Vidal, p. 84.
24. Ibid., p. 32.
25. Ibid., p. 34.
26. Ibid., p. 312.
27. Ibid.
28. Ibid., 165-166.
29. Ibid., p. 35.
30. Ibid.
31. Ibid., p. 166.
32. Ibid., p. 166.
33. Ibid., 34-35.
34. Ibid., p. 166.
35. Dick, *The Apostate Angel*, p. 13.
36. Vidal, *The Last Empire*, p. 115.
37. Vidal, *Palimpsest*, p. 174.
38. Vidal, *The Last Empire*, p. 115.
39. Vidal, *At Home*, p. 289.
40. Vidal, *Palimpsest*, p. 169. Surprisingly, in light of his

friendship with Gore Vidal and being in Paris at the same time, there is no evidence that Tennessee Williams ever met Denham Fouts.

41. Bucknell, *Christopher Isherwood Diaries*, p. 401.
42. Ibid.
43. Isherwood, *My Guru and His Disciple*, p. 194.
44. Vidal, *Palimpsest*, p. 176.
45. Plimpton, *Truman Capote*, p. 89.
46. Vidal, *Palimpsest*, p. 179.
47. Ibid., pp. 179, 180.
48. Ibid., p. 180.
49. Plimpton, p. 89.
50. Bucknell, p. 402.
51. Vidal, *Palimpsest*, p. 179.
52. Ibid., p. 180.
53. Bucknell, p. 402.
54. Bucknell, *Christopher Isherwood: Lost Years*, p. 142.
55. Ibid., p. 142.
56. Isherwood, , p. 142.
57. Ibid., p. 142.
58. Isherwood, *Down There on a Visit*, pp. 305, 306.
59. Plimpton, p. 88.
60. Bucknell, p. 402.
61. Plimpton, p. 89.
62. Stanton, *Views from a Window*, p. 92.
63. Ibid., p. 93.
64. Wishart, *High Diver*, p. 60.
65. Vidal, *The Judgment of Paris*, p. 568.
66. Ibid.
67. Ibid., p. 569.
68. Ibid., p. 568.
69. Ibid., p. 569.
70. Ibid., p. 570.
71. Ibid.
72. Ibid., p. 571.

73. Ibid.
74. Ibid., p. 572.
75. Ibid.
76. Ibid., p. 598.
77. Ibid., p. 600.
78. Vidal, *Palimpsest*, p. 100.
79. Stanton, pp. 57-58.
80. Vidal, *A Thirsty Evil*, p. 97.
81. Ibid., p. 101.
82. Ibid., p. 100.
83. Ibid., p. 101.
84. Ibid.
85. Ibid., p. 102.
86. Ibid., p. 103.
87. Ibid., p. 104.
88. Ibid., pp. 104-105.
89. Ibid., p. 108.
90. Ibid.
91. Ibid., p. 105.
92. Wishart, p. 54.
93. Vidal, *Palimpsest*, p. 180.
94. Vidal, *A Thirsty Evil*, p. 111.
95. Ibid., p. 112.
96. Vidal, *Palimpsest*, p. 155.
97. Vidal, *A Thirsty Evil*, p. 113.
98. Ibid., p. 114.
99. Ibid.
100.   Ibid., p. 115.
101.   Ibid., p. 114.
102.   Ibid., p. 116.
103.   Ibid., p. 117.
104.   Ibid., p. 118.
105.   Ibid., p. 120.
106.   Ibid.
107.   Vidal, *The Last Empire*, p. 308

CHAPTER SEVEN

1. Clarke, *Capote*, pp. 164-165.
2. Ibid., p. 166. The reconciliation between Watson and Hansen didn't last too long. On July 15, 1949, Capote would write to a friend: "do you remember Waldemar Hansen? I saw him in Paris and he is a wreck: the poor thing has been ousted by Peter Watson, and it is one of the most fabulous stories you've ever heard." In a letter a month later he filled in the details. "Peter Watson ran off with someone else, a brickhead from California who had been Waldemar's lover before he met Peter and who W had rejected in favor of Mr. Watson! How's that for irony?" Clarke, *Too Brief a Treat*, p. 94, p. 98.
3. Ibid., p. 174.
4. Capote, *Answered Prayers*, p. 26.
5. Capote, *Portraits and Observations*, p. 301.
6. Clarke, *Capote*, p. 176.
7. Vidal, *Palimpsest*, p. 180.
8. Capote, *Answered Prayers*, p. 32.
9. Clarke, *Capote*, p. 173.
10. Capote, *Answered Prayers*, p. 29.
11. Ibid., pp. 32-33.
12. Clarke, *Capote*, 174.
13. Capote, *Answered Prayers*, p. 36.
14. Capote, *Answered Prayers*, p. 85.
15. Clarke, *Capote*, p. 174.
16. Capote, *Answered Prayers*, p. 35.
17. Ibid., p. 66. This story must have haunted Capote. He wrote a longer version of it as a chapter for *Answered Prayers*, "Mojave," but then took it out and made it the fourth chapter of *Music for Chameleons*. Capote, *Three by*

Truman Capote, p. 208 et seq.

18. Rorem, *A Ned Rorem Reader*, p. 275.
19. Capote, *Portraits and Observations*, p. 301.
20. Clarke, *Too Brief a Treat*, p. 258.
21. Bucknell, *Christopher Isherwood: Lost Years*, p. 119.
22. Berg, *Conversations with Christopher Isherwood*, p. 17.
23. Clarke, *Capote*, p. 314.
24. Grobel, *Conversations with Capote*, p. 199.
25. Clarke, *Capote*, p. 491.
26. Ibid., p. 317.
27. Plimpton, *Truman Capote*, p. 197.
28. Grobel, p. 112.
29. Clarke, p. 318.
30. Ibid., p. 323.
31. Ibid., p. 330.
32. Clarke, *Too Brief a Treat*, p. 287.
33. Werth, *The Scarlet Professor*, p. 253.
34. Clarke, *Too Brief a Treat*, p. 296.
35. Grobel, p. 79.
36. Ibid., p. 111.
37. Clarke, *Too Brief a Treat*, p. 335.
38. Clarke, *Capote*, p. 325.
39. Clarke, *Too Brief a Treat*, p. 340.
40. Ibid., p. 413.
41. Ibid., p. 421.
42. Plimpton, p. 249.
43. Ibid., p. 248.
44. Ibid., p. 269.
45. Grobel, p. 117.
46. Clarke, *Capote*, p. 320.
47. Ibid., pp. 399-400.
48. Ibid., p. 398.
49. Plimpton, p. 176.
50. Clarke, *Capote*, p. 405.
51. Ibid., p. 311.

52. Grobel, p. 222.
53. Capote, *Three by Truman Capote*, p. 193.
54. Grobel, p. 231.
55. Clarke, *Too Brief a Treat*, p. 448.
56. Clarke, *Capote*, p. 155.
57. Ibid., p. 485.
58. Capote, *Answered Prayers*, p. 5.
59. Ibid., p. 35.
60. Ibid., p. 22.
61. Ibid., p. 21.
62. Ibid., p. 23.
63. Ibid., p. 24.
64. Ibid., p. 25.
65. Ibid., p. 26.
66. Ibid.
67. Ibid., pp. 26-27.
68. Ibid., p. 26.
69. Ibid., p. 27.
70. Ibid., pp. 29-30.
71. Ibid., p. 30.
72. Ibid., p. 36.
73. Ibid., p. 29.
74. Ibid., pp. 33-34.
75. Ibid., p. 34.
76. Ibid., p. 36.
77. Ibid., p. 67.
78. Ibid., p. 96.
79. Plimpton, p. 446.
80. Capote, *Three by Truman Capote*, p. 192.
81. Ibid., p. 193.
82. Clarke, *Capote*, p. 491.
83. Plimpton, pp. 446-447.
84. Ibid., pp 449-451. Gore Vidal had his own cynical take on it: "Mr. Capote never wrote *Answered Prayers*. It is the Madonna of the Future all over again. But as this is

America, if you publicize a nonexistent work enough, it becomes positively palpable. It would be nice if he were to get the Nobel on the strength of *Answered Prayers*, which he, indeed, never wrote. There were a few jagged pieces of what might have been a gossip-novel published in *Esquire*. The rest is silence; and litigation and ...noise on TV." Grobel, p. 201. In 1978, Truman had remarked to his friend of three decades, Donald Windham, "Well, even if I never finished Answered Prayers, it's better known than most books that are published." Windham thought to himself that Truman "had created another category: the non-written novel." Windham, *Lost Friendships*, p. 154.
85. Capote, *Answered Prayers*, p. 100.

CHAPTER EIGHT

1. Wishart, *High Diver*, p. 59.
2. Ibid., p. 60.
3. Ford, *Water from a Bucket*, p. 4.
4. Shelden, *Friends of Promise*, pp. 203-204.
5. Lancaster, *Brian Howard*, pp. 289-290.
6. Ibid., p. 280.
7. Shelden, p. 208.
8. Ibid., pp. 204-205.
9. Bucknell, *Christopher Isherwood: Lost Years*, p. 300; Clarke, *Capote: A Biography*, p. 174.
10. Bucknell, *Christopher Isherwood: Lost Years*, pp. 172-3.
11. Richard Wall, "The World's Most Expensive Male Prostitute." *Folio Weekly*, (Jacksonville, Florida), June 12, 2012.
12. Leddick, *Intimate Companions*, p. 207.
13. Huntington Library, Letter of Glenway Wescott to Christopher Isherwood, December 25, 1948, Christopher

Isherwood Papers.

14. Phelps and Rosco, *Continual Lessons*, p. 211.
15. *Op cit supra* note 12.
16. Clarke, 174.
17. Clarke, 173.
18. Shelden, p. 208.
19. Ellman, *Oscar Wilde*, p. 74.
20. Wishart, p. 58.
21. Ibid., p. 60.
22. The account of Elliott Magren's death in Gore Vidal's "Pages from An Abandoned Journal" follows precisely Denny's death: Elliott was found "face down in the bathroom, dead. When the autopsy was performed, it was discovered that Elliott had had a malformed heart, an extremely rare case, and he might have died as suddenly at any moment in his life ... He was buried Christmas Day in the Protestant cemetery close to Shelley, in good company to the end." Vidal, *A Thirsty Evil*, p. 121.
23. Wishart, p. 60.
24. Huntington Library, Letter of Glenway Wescott to Christopher Isherwood, early March 1949.
25. Bucknell, *Christopher Isherwood Diaries*, p. 409.
26. Ibid., p. 460.
27. Plimpton, (editor), *Writers of Work*, 4th Series, p. 222. Ibid, p. 550.
28. Bucknell, *Christopher Isherwood Diaries*, p. 834.
29. Wishart, p. 54.
30. Ibid., p. 54.

BIBLIOGRAPHY

Baker, Susan and Curtis S. Gibson. *Gore Vidal: A Critical Companion*. Westport, Connecticut: Greenwood Press, 1997.

Beaton, Cecil. *Cecil Beaton: Memoirs of the 40's*. New York: McGraw-Hill Book Company, 1972.

Beaton, Cecil. *The Wandering Years. Diaries: 1922-1939*. Boston: Little, Brown and Company, 1961.

Bell, Anne Olivier. (editor). *The Diary of Virginia Woolf*. Volume One: 1915-1919. New York: Harcourt Brace & Company, 1977.

Benkovitz, Miriam J. *Ronald Firbank: A Biography*. New York: Alfred A. Knopf, 1969.

Berg, James J. and Chris Freeman, (editors). *Conversations with Christopher Isherwood*. Jackson, Mississippi: University Press of Mississippi, 2001.

Booth, Martin. *Opium: A History*. New York: St. Martin's Griffin, 1996.

Bowles, Paul. *Without Stopping: An Autobiography*. Hopewell, New Jersey: The Ecco Press, 1972.

Bradford, Sarah. *The Reluctant King: The Life and Reign of George VI*. New York: St. Martin's Press, 1989.

Brophy, Brigid. *Prancing Novelist: A Defense of Fiction in the Form of a Critical Biography in Praise of Ronald Firbank*. New York: Harper & Row, 1973.

Buckle, Richard (editor). *Self Portrait With Friends: The Selected Diaries of Cecil Beaton: 1926-1974*. New York: Times Books, 1979.

175

Bucknell, Katherine (editor). *Christopher Isherwood Diaries: Volume One: 1939-1960*. New York: Michael di Capua Books, HarperCollins Publishers, 1996.

Bucknell, Katherine (editor). *Christopher Isherwood: Lost Years: A Memoir 1945-1951*. New York: HarperCollins Publishers, 2000.

Caponi, Gena Dagel. *Paul Bowles: Romantic Savage*. Carbondale, Illinois. Southern University Press, 1994.

Capote, Truman. *Answered Prayers: The Unfinished Novel*. New York: Random House, 1987.

_____. *Portraits and Observations: The Essays of Truman Capote*. New York; Random House, 2007.

_____. *Selected Writings*. New York: The Modern Library, 1959.

_____. *Three by Truman Capote: Other Voices, Other Rooms, Breakfast at Tiffany's, Music for Chameleons*. New York: Random House, 1985.

Carr, Virginia Spencer. *Paul Bowles: A Life*. New York: Scribner, 2004.

Ceresi, Frank and Mark Rucker. *Baseball in Washington, D.C.* Charleston, South Carolina: Arcadia Publishing, 2002.

Cheever, Susan. *Desire: Where Sex Meets Addiction*. New York: Simon & Schuster Paperbacks, 2008.

Chisholm, Anne. *Nancy Cunard: A Biography*. Middlesex, England: Penguin Books Ltd., 1981.

Clarke, Gerald (editor). *Too Brief a Treat: The Letters of Truman Capote*. New York: Random House, 2004.

Clarke, Gerald. *Capote: A Biography*. New York: Simon and Schuster, 1988.

Connolly, Cressida. *The Rare and the Beautiful: The Art, Loves, and Lives of the Garman Sisters*. New York: Harper Collins Publishers, 2004.

Cowley, Malcolm (editor). *Writers at Work: The Paris Review Interviews*. First Series. New York: Penguin Books, 1986.

Davis, Deborah, *Party of the Century: The Fabulous Story of Truman Capote and His Black and White Ball*. New York: John Wiley & Sons, Inc., 2006.

Devlin, Albert J. and Tischler, Nancy M., (editors). *The Selected Letters of Tennessee Williams: Volume I, 1920-1945*. New York: New Directions Publishing Corporation, New York, 2000.

Devlin, Albert J. (editor), Tischler, Nancy M. (co-editor). *The Selected Letters of Tennessee Williams: Volume II, 1945-1957*. New York: New Directions Publishing Corporation, 2004.

Dick, Bernard F. *The Apostate Angel: A Critical Study of Gore Vidal*. New York: Random House, 1974.

Dunphy, Jack. *"Dear Genius . . .": A Memoir of My Life with Truman Capote*. New York: McGraw-Hill Book Company, 1987.

Dwyer, Michael Middleton (editor). *Great Houses of the Hudson River*. New York: AOL Time Warner Book Group, 2003.

Ellman, Richard. *Oscar Wilde*. New York: Alfred A. Knopf, 1988.

Etcoff, Nancy. *Survival of the Prettiest: The Science of Beauty*. New York: Anchor Books, 1999.

Finney, Brian. *Christopher Isherwood: A Critical Biography*. New York: Oxford University Press, 1979.

Fisher, Clive. *Cyril Connolly: The Life and Times of England's Most Controversial Literary Critic*. New York: St. Martin's Press, 1995.

Ford, Charles Henri. *Water from a Bucket: A Diary: 1948-1957*. New York: Turtle Point Press, 2001.

Ford, Hugh (editor). *Nancy Cunard: Brave Poet, Indomitable Rebel: 1896-1965*. Philadelphia: Chilton Book Company, 1968.

Geiger, John. *Nothing is True Everything is Permitted: The Life of Brion Gysin*. New York: The Disinformation Company Ltd., 2005.

Gill, Brendan. *Here at the New Yorker*. New York: Carroll & Gaf Publishers, Inc., 1987.

Goldsmith, John (editor). *Stephen Spender, Journals: 1939-1983*. New York: Random House, 1986.

Gordon, Lois. *Nancy Cunard: Heiress, Muse, Political Idealist*. New York: Columbia University Press, 2007.

Graves, Robert and Alan Hodge. *The Long Week End: A Social History of Great Britain: 1918-1939*. New York: The Macmillan Company, 1941.

Grobel, Lawrence. *Conversations with Capote*. New York: New American Library, 1985.

Guggenheim, Peggy. *Confessions of an Art Addict*. New York: The Macmillan Company, 1960.

Hewison, Robert. *Under Siege: Literary Life in London: 1939-45*. New York: Oxford University Press, 1977.

Hibbard, Allen. *Paul Bowles Magic & Morocco*. San Francisco: Cadmus Editions, 2004.

Hoare, Philip. *Serious Pleasures: The Life of Stephen Tennant*. London: Hamish Hamilton, 1990.

Hyde, H. Montgomery. *Lord Alfred Douglas: A Biography*. New York: Dodd, Mead & Company, 1984.

Isherwood, Christopher. *Christopher and His Kind: 1929-1939*. New York: Farrar, Straus & Giroux, 1976.

_____. *Down There on a Visit*. New York: A Bard Book, Avon Books, 1978.

_____. *Lions and Shadows: An Education in the Twenties*. New York: Pegasus, 1969.

_____. *October*. Los Angeles: Twelvetress Press, 1981.

_____. *My Guru and His Disciple*. New York: Farrar, Straus & Giroux, 1980.

_____. *Kathleen and Frank: The Autobiography of a Family*. New York: Simon and Schuster, 1971.

Jenrette, Richard Hampton. *Adventures with Old Houses*. Charleston: Wyrick & Company, 2000.

John, Augustus. *Chiaroscuro: Fragments of Autobiography*. London: Jonathan Cape, 1954.

Kaczynski, Richard. *Perdurabo: The Life of Aleister Crowley*. Tempe, Arizona: New Falcon Publications, 2002.

Kaplan, Fred. *Gore Vidal: A Biography*. New York: Doubleday, 1999.

Keith, Slim (with Annette Tapert). *Slim: Memories of a Rich and Imperfect Life*. New York: Simon and Schuster, 1990.

Kuri, Jose Ferez (editor). *Brion Gysin: Tuning in to the Multimedia Age*. London: Thames & Hudson, Ltd., 2003.

Lambert, Gavin. *Norman's Letter*. New York: Coward-McCann, Inc., 1966.

Lancaster, Marie-Jaqueline: *Brian Howard: Portrait of a Failure*. United Kingdom: Green Candy Press, 2007.

Leavitt, Richard F. (editor). *The World of Tennessee Williams*. New York: G.P. Putnam's Sons, 1978.

Leddick, David. *Intimate Companions: A Triography of George Platt Lynes, Paul Cadmus, Lincoln Kirstein, and Their Circle*. New York: St. Martin's Press, 2000.

Lehmann, John. *In My Own Time: Memoirs of a Literary Life*. Boston: Little, Brown and Company, 1969.

_____. *The Whispering Gallery: Autobiography I*. New York: Harcourt, Brace and Company, 1955.

Leverich, Lyle. *Tom: The Unknown Tennessee Williams*. New York: Crown, Publishers, Inc., 1995.

Lewis, Jeremy. *Cyril Connolly: A Life*. London, Pimlico, 1997.

Long, Gregory. *Historic Houses of the Hudson River Valley: 1663-1915*. New York: Rizzoli International Publications, Inc., 2004.

Maugham, W. Somerset. *The Razor's Edge*. New York: Vintage Books, 1972.

Meyers, Jeffrey. *Somerset Maugham: A Life*. New York: Alfred A. Knopf, 2004.

Montgomery-Massingberd, Hugh and Sykes, Christopher Simon. *Great Houses of England and Wales*. London, Laurence King Publishing, Ltd., 1994.

Murray, Douglas. *Bosie: A Biography of Lord Alfred Douglas*. New York: Hyperion, 2000.

Murray, Nicholas. *Aldous Huxley: A Biography*. New York: St. Martin's Press, 2002.

Nicolson, Nigel (editor). *Harold Nicolson: The Later Years: 1945-1962*. New York: Atheneum, 1968.

Nicolson, Nigel. *Long Life: Memoirs*. New York: G.P. Putnam's Sons, 1998.

Parini, Jay (editor). *Gore Vidal: Writer Against the Grain*. New York: Columbia University Press, 1992.

Parker, Peter. *Isherwood: A Life Revealed*. New York: Random House, 2004.

Phelps, Robert, with Jerry Rosco, (editors). *Continual Lessons: The Journals of Glenway Wescott, 1937-1955*. New York: Farrar, Straus & Giroux, 1990.

Plimpton, George, editor. *Truman Capote: In Which Various Friends, Enemies, Acquaintances and Detractors Recall His Turbulent Career*. New York: Nan A. Talese Doubleday, 1997.

Plimpton, George (editor). *Writers at Work: The Paris Review Interviews*. Fourth Series. New York: Penguin Books, 1987.

_____ (editor). *Writers at Work: The Paris Review Interviews*. Fifth Series. New York: Penguin Books, 1987.

_____ (editor). *Writers at Work: The Paris Review Interviews*. Sixth Series. New York: Penguin Books, 1985.

Powell, Anthony. *To Keep the Ball Rolling: The Memoirs of Anthony Powell*. Chicago: The University of Chicago Press, 1983.

Pryce-Jones, David. *The Bonus of Laughter*. London: Hamish Hamilton, 1987.

_____. *Cyril Connolly: Journal and Memoir.* New York: Ticknor & Fields, 1984.

Queen Frederica of the Hellenes. *A Measure of Understanding.* New York: St. Martin's Press, 1971.

Rader, Dotson. *Tennessee: Cry of the Heart.* New York: Doubleday & Company, Inc., 1985.

Roberts, James C. *Hardball on the Hill: Baseball Stories from Our Nation's Capital.* Chicago: Triumph Books, 2001.

Robertson, Sandy. *The Illustrated Beast: The Aleister Crowley Scrapbook.* Boston: Weiser Books, 1988.

Rorem, Ned. *A Ned Rorem Reader.* New Haven: Yale University Press, 2001.

Sawyer-Laucanno, Christopher. *An Invisible Spectator: A Biography of Paul Bowles.* New York: Grove Press, 1989.

Shelden, Michael. *Friends of Promise: Cyril Connolly and the World of Horizon.* New York: Harper & Row, Publishers, 1989.

Skelton, Barbara. *Tears Before Bedtime and Weep No More.* London, Pimlica, 1993.

Smith, Barry (editor). *The Collected Letters of Peter Warlock (Philip Heseltine).* Woodbridge, Suffolks, United Kingdom: The Boydell Press, 2005.

Smith, Barry. *Peter Warlock: The Life of Philip Heseltine.* Oxford: Oxford University Press, 1994.

Spender, Stephen. *The Thirties and After: Poetry, Politics, People: 1933-1970.* New York: Random House, 1978.

Spender, Stephen. *World Within World.* New York: Harcourt, Brace and Company, 1951.

Stanton, Robert J. (editor). *Views from a Window: Conversations with Gore Vidal.* Secaucus, New Jersey: Lyle Stuart Inc., 1980.

Sutherland, John. *Stephen Spender: A Literary Life.* New York: Oxford University Press, 2005.

Sutin, Lawrence. *A Life of Aleister Crowley.* New York: St. Martin's Griffin, 2000.

Symonds, John. *The Beast 666: The Life of Aleister Crowley.* London: Pindar Press, 1997.
_____. *The Great Beast: The Life and Magick of Aleister Crowley.* Great Britain: Mayflower Books Ltd., 1973.

Taylor, D.J. *Bright Young People: The Lost Generation of London's Jazz Age.* New York: Farrar, Straus and Giroux, 2007.

Thornton, Margaret Bradham (editor). *Notebooks: Tennessee Williams.* New Haven: Yale University Press, 2006.

Van der Kiste, John. *Kings of the Hellenes: The Greek Kings: 1863-1974.* Dover, New Hampshire: Alan Sutton Publishing Inc., 1994.

Vickers, Hugo. *Cecil Beaton: A Biography.* Boston: Little, Brown and Company, 1985.

Vidal, Gore. *At Home: Essays 1982-1988.* New York: Random House, 1988.
_____. *Julian. Williwaw. The Judgment of Paris. Messiah. The City and the Pillar.* New York: Ocotopus/Heinemann, 1979.
_____. *The Last Empire. Essays: 1991-2000.* New York: Doubleday, 2001.
_____. *Palimpsest: A Memoir.* New York: Random House, 1995.
_____. *Point to Point Navigation: A Memoir.* New York. Doubleday, 2006.
_____. *Screening History.* Cambridge, Harvard University Press, 1992.
_____. *Snapshots in History's Glare.* New York: Abrams, 2009.
_____. *A Thirsty Evil: Seven Short Stories.* New York: Signet Books, The New American Library, 1956.
_____. *United States: Essays 1952-1992.* New York: Random House, 1993.

Washington, Peter. *Madame Blavatsky's Baboon: A History of the Mystics, Mediums, and Misfits Who Brought Spiritualism to America.* New York: Schocken Books, 1995.

Weise, Donald (editor). *Gore Vidal: Sexually Speaking; Collected Sex Writings.* San Francisco: Cleis Press, Inc., 1999.

Werth, Barry. *The Scarlet Professor: Newton Arvin: A Literary Life Shattered by Scandal.* New York: Doubleday, 2001.

West, Nigel. *MI5: British Security Service Operations 1909-1945.* New York: Stein and Day, 1981.

Williams, Tennessee. *Memoirs.* New York: Anchor Press/ Doubleday, 1983.

_____. *Where I Live: Selected Essays.* New York: A New Directions Book, 1978.

Windham, Donald. *Footnote to a Friendship: A Memoir of Truman Capote and Others.* Privately printed, 1983.

_____. *Lost Friendships: A Memoir of Truman Capote, Tennessee Williams and Others.* New York: William Morrow and Company, Inc., 1987

Windham, Donald (editor). *Tennessee Williams' Letters to Donald Windham: 1940-1965.* New York: Holt, Rinehart and Winston, 1977.

Wishart, Michael. *High Diver.* London: Blond & Briggs Ltd., 1977.

MANUSCRIPT COLLECTIONS

Papers of Sir Cecil Beaton, St. John's College Library, University of Cambridge

Papers of Gore Vidal, Houghton Library, Harvard College Library, Cambridge, Massachusetts

Papers of Truman Capote, Archival Collection, Neilson Library, Smith College, Northampton, Massachusetts

Papers of Truman Capote, The New York Public Library, Manuscripts and Archives Division, New York, New York

Papers of Truman Capote, Yale Collection of American Literature, Beinecke Rare Book and Manuscript Collection, New Haven, Connecticut

Papers of Evan Morgan, Lord Tredegar, National Library of Wales

Christopher Isherwood Papers, The Huntington Library, San Marino, California

The Cyril Connolly Papers, McFarlin Library, University of Tulsa, Department of Special Collections, Tulsa, Oklahoma

ABOUT THE AUTHOR

A graduate of Wesleyan University and University of Virginia School of Law, Arthur Vanderbilt is the author of many books of history, biography, memoirs, and essays. His books have been selections of the Book-of-the-Month Club, *Readers Digest's* "Today's Best Nonfiction," the Easton Press series, and other book clubs, and have been serialized in newspapers and magazines, both here and abroad, translated into foreign languages, excerpted for anthologies, and optioned for television movies. He lives in New Jersey and Massachusetts.

16164522R00108

Made in the USA
Middletown, DE
06 December 2014